TANGSHAN EARTHQUAKE

-A FUNERAL ORATION TO THE TENTH ANNIVERSARY OF THE DISASTER ON JULY 28TH

WRITTEN BY **QIANGANG**
TRANSLATED BY **WANG ZHENGNIAN**

Preface by the Translator

Do you know some earthquake by undergoing it as a refugee or relief personnel? Do you remember the Tangshan Earthquake happened in Tangshan city, Hebei province, the People' Republic of China on July 28th, 1976, which murdered 240,000 lives, created more than 1000, 000 heavy wounded people, also uncountable light wounded ones; which smashed 95 percent of the housing areas of the city; which of course was the most serious affecting earthquake in this century. No, in the history of human being; which…
A talent Chinese young writer wrote down this reportage at the eve of the tenth anniversary to this grand earthquake, which collects full first hand materials from the victims and witnesses who saw, underwent the very process of the disaster; which describes those survivors spending their evil time in the ruins for three days, eight days, thirteen days, the longest fifteen days without food and water; which has both abundant datum and profound learning and thinking, which tells us the story why the Chinese seismologists failed to forecast the catastrophe and what they did before and after the earthquake; which…

Reading such a historical reportage is worthy and valuable. Seeing believes, read it, my dear reader.

Translator Wang Zhengnian

Tangshan Earthquake

-A Funeral Oration to the Tenth Anniversary Of The Disaster On July 28^{th,} 1976

Written By Qian Gang

Translated By Wang Zhengnian

Content

 About Tangshan and I
Chapter I Falling Day July 28th
.3 o'clock 42 minutes 53 seconds
. Having Been Warned By Nature
. Words of Those Eyewitnesses
The Dying Morning

Chapter II Tang Shan –Hiroshima

. The Red Ambulance
. The Dohe River, The Dohe River
. Kailuan Coal Mine, Kailuan Coal Mine
. Destination-Tangshan
. City in Severe Pain
. Above and Under The Ground
. Save Those Lives

Chapter III Life Seekers

Three Days: A Couple and A Kitchen Knife
. Eight Days: "Little Girl" Wang Zilan
. Thirteen Days: A Woman Surpassing The Limit of Life
. Fifteen Days: Last Five Men

Chapter IV In Another World

. Hotels
. Lockup
. Psychiatric Hospital
. Inhabitant District Of Those Blinds
. Chapter V uneven August
. Release of The Criminal Energy
. Push Away Pestilence

. Anecdote Have Ark
. Political 1976

Chapter VI Those Orphans

. 3,000 –Unfortunate Survivors
. Five Sisters and Brothers Named Zhang

Chapter VII State Seismic Bureau Before And After The Earthquake

."Starve Them To Death"
."Let Them Pain To Death"
."Shoot Them To Death"
. In The State Seismic Bureau On July 28th

. Memorandum (I)

. Memorandum (II)

. History Remembers The Them

My Concluding Remarks

Devote This Funeral Oration To My Beloved Tangshan

. About My Tangshan and I
Doubtlessly Tangshan belongs to me.
Supposing ten years ago, this 23 years old young man, his foot in chamois leather boots, carrying the hand operated sprayer on his shoulder, in the white gown of the epidemic prevention team, walking about the shaking-world ruins day by day, when I came to Tangshan again and said farewell again, I am conscious that I can no longer depart from Tangshan.

Not long ago, I found a "Today in the World History" at Xinhuan bookstore with one of my friends, immediately I took it down the bookshelf, almost unconsciously I turned it to the page.
Yes, this is the day when is certain to be written in black print;
July 28th
In 1794, French revolutionaries Roberts.Bill and Saint.Justus were executed to death,
In 1914, Austro-Hungary Empire declared war to Serbia, the First World War broke out,
In 1937, Japanese occupied Peking,

In 1973, French burst the second atomic bomb on coral reef,

In 1976, grand Earthquake shock Tangshan.

I saw my Tangshan, my disaster-ridden Tangshan, and my scarred Tangshan, who narrowly escaped from death in the catastrophe. Reasonably, Tangshan earthquake should be remembered by human beings together with all the events in the world history in the development of man.

The Tangshan people will never forgot this anniversary. During these years every dawn on July 28th comes to man, some shadows of people are dragging in the streets in Tangshan. A cluster and cluster fire lights up in violate silence, in the light of the flame one another pairs of eyes are reflected; of those old, of those mid-ages, also was reflected those lit-up paper-made cashes in their hands.

To my son XXX

To my lovable daughter XXX;

To my father and mother.

In the first ray of the morning sun the smoke produced by the light yellowish paper made coins resembled to a stretch of white strip, like fog floating among the newly built high-rises. The paper coins floated in the white fog, like one another black butterflies in the sights of children, flying very high and falling down slowly, falling down into the grass beside the walkways, falling down on the silverfish-hair temples of those old women standing in the street, who did not tap it off, whose eyes were staring at the ground boldly, no, not to the ground but the world under the ground. Their lips were trembling, seeming murmuring something.

I have passed these paper coin-floating streets again and again. I know those dead men killed by July 28th earthquake have no their graveyards in Tangshan; those road-crosses under the high-rises, those old narrow lanes, those piled-up hills after the earthquake, even those newly decided sites of workshops are their graveyards without tombstones. Ten years ago, it was at these spots they were stroke down by the beams of houses, crashed by the slabs of buildings, or buried and suffocated by the debris and rubbish. Ten years later, those ruins are no longer existing, however I recognize all these. I walked from the newly built leading roads lined by young trees in diameter of a fist to the old roads lined by old trees. It was a night without moon, wandering on a pavement having been walked ten years ago, I found suddenly those high old white poplars under the streetlights, with silver-white throughout their bodies, glittering wonderful light. Are those poplars, which shook fiercely like masts of boats in waves, these old trees that had witnessed the terrible scene at the moment still silently, loyally safeguarding something? Those zigzag branches of these poplars reminds people thinking of their thick roots. For ten years, are these roots of the old poplars, which stretch their roots deeply into the ground where dead men sleep forever; did they transmit some message to those on and under the ground? To those lives and the dead?

Tangshan earthquake is the most miserable page in the world earthquake history so far. The book "The Shaking Of The Earth" published by the Seismic Publishing House, China, published to the world this extremely tragic fact,

Dead men 242,769 person;

Heavy wounded people: 164,851 people.

Each time I read these figures, I feel my heart clutched again and again.

The situation of Tokyo 8.2 degrees earthquake on Sept. 1st 1923 was extremely terrible, the sub-disaster caused by the earthquake-- fire burned almost half of Tokyo, those dead accounted only ten thousand or so.

The 8.5 degrees of Chile earthquake occurred on May 22nd, 1960 caused tsunami sweeping the Pacific Ocean, and the seismic sea wave drove straight toward Japan, which tossed the fish boat to the roof on the coastal houses. The dead of this earthquake accounted to a total of 7,000.

Again the Alaska 8.4 degrees earthquake, USA happened on March 28th, 1964, together with ice slide, landslide, tsunami and mud eruption killed a total of 178 people.

What do these figures mean? That means: the figure of dead in Tangshan earthquake is equivalent to 2.4 times of that of the world-shaking Tokyo earthquake; 3.5 times to that of Chile's; more than 1,300 times to that of Alaska.

The more important is the miserable fate behind these figures. Man can account the losses of material wealth by billions, or ten of billions. By what can they account the losses of man? Those living people are unaccountable.

Too hard, it was too hard to forget all these.

Not long ago, I visited a woman from Tangshan. In her home she served me both fruits and candy. I invited her to have some politely. She refused by waving her hand constantly," No, no." she said, "I have not had anything sweet after the earthquake." She told me that the first thing she had been a bottle of grape sugar water when she was rescued after being buried in the ruin for two days and nights. Afterwards, anything sweet such as an apple, an orange, even sweet dumpling (yuanxiao) will cause her strong reaction of deadly thirsty experienced in the ruin ten years ago. "I can't withstand it". For ten years the taste of bitterness has not left her. Never has it!

"Those who underwent the earthquake seemed to have suffered from a severe sickness." Another woman said to me," Every time it is cloudy, or it is getting dark, I feel nameless bad, I have my chest depressed and can not breath, I always breath heavily, trying to run out of the room…" She has run out of her room once and again, whether it was snowing or west cold wind was blowing hard, despite of her husband's persuasion, she refused to return to her home. She was frightened! She was rescued three days after being buried in the ruin and still remembered the fashion of the black hell, which imprisoned her for three days. Whenever it is getting dark, that horrible and depressing sensation will catch her, suffocating her. It has been for more than ten years, what unshaped thing is still torturing this weak woman cruelly?

A mid-aged teacher, his tone was very calm, however with sorrow penetrating his calm," We have forgot those sorrowful things, forgot, has forgotten…" Do they really forget? At the moment, in order to save his wife, he had been raking the ruin for a whole day. It was a big fire that ended up his hope. He told me that his wife was burned in that ruin. He fell faint at the very site. How can he forget all these? That was a terrible fire. During my call someone has rolled up his sleeves, pointing to the scar in the arm, he told me, the fire flamed the bodies of his kinsfolk, the scar was burned by the boiled oil of MAN.

There was also he, the old man Liu Gu, sitting in his silent cold home, seeing him pretending delightful smile, I truly wanted to cry, "In the night of the earthquake, I was in Tianjin for business and was called up my family at ten that night. The call was answered by my youngest daughter, who asked me," Daddy, have you bought me the sandals? I said, "Yes, I have". She asked me again, "Are they silver-gray?" I said, "Yes". She asked me whether the sandals were good looking or not and required me to bring her as soon as possible…" He could not go on, tears of the old man came down the wrinkles over his face. It has been for ten years, he was still reserving that pair of silver-gray sandals, like reserving his daughter's vivid beauty-loving heart…
Those 240,000 souls seemed leaving us one by one like that.

The 255 Army Hospital was my residence to this Tangshan tour where 400 died of the disaster out of her total personnel of 1,200. There was a small mourning hall in the hospital, remaining the cinerary caskets of some of the dead men. When I came into the small room lit mutely, my chest was plugged. All the photos on the cinerary caskets, all those pairs of eyes were alive, were alive.
A young nurse wearing a pigtail wore a set of washed uniform, a visor-cap on her head, carrying a big size badge of Mao Tse-tong, all of which printed the color of the era, only her charming smile was over the time. Therefore today, ten years later, when I saw this photo, a romantic idea came to me, supposing she had sent some photo to her lover, it must be this one.

I can simply watch the boy who had a peaked-cap and a pair of extremely lovable big eyes, on his cinerary casket, a small flower ring was placed, it was written on the elegiac couplet, "May you rest in peace, Han Zhi. Your father and mother."

There was another flower ring beside, on which there was similar writing, "May you rest in peace, Han Song. By Your father and mother". The younger brother was a more lovable boy, losing such a pair of boys. I cannot imagine upon what these parent can depend to support their life and feeling.
The loss was too heavy. In the small mourning hall I not only read the written by tears, but also hear clearly the sorrowful and constant crying of these pitiful parents.

On the cinerary casket of a little girl, there was a pack of unpacked chocolate, which has melted. The pitiful girl probably has not had what she liked as much as she would when she was alive. However everything was irretrievable. This was the tragedy that the nature imposed on man.

There was also a special big sized cinerary casket, which consists of one big, and three small caskets. This was really a special pattern and was made by a father. It symbolized a mother and three of their kids passing away human society. I cannot imagine what his feeling was when the father of the kids manufactured the caskets. The kids have left accessing their mother and left him alone. Who on earth the most unfortunate one, those dead people, or the alive?

There was a small hill outside the mourning hall mounted by the broken walls, debris, and fragments of the bricks, rubble of roofs raked out of the ruins after the earthquake. There were stairs, wayside pavilion and playing children upon it, those children born after the earthquake without undergoing the disaster. Among the flaws of the debris a stick of another rusty reinforce steel bar stretched out, the bent broken water pipe, or pipes of heater. Standing beside these I seemed to be at a black, deadly silent sea, listening to the various signals from the extremely deep underground, those weak however produced-by-man signals. Those 240,000 living souls, they cursed, cried, entreated and moaned at the moment; when their lives were torn, they had no time to think over, to deliberate, to hide, to escape, were broken up from this bright world; becoming the life-prisoners in the depth underground. I thought of those artless ad innocent children in the mourning hall, perhaps because of their existing every inch of land under my feet was twitching painfully.

This is my Tangshan.

Ten years ago, when I, an innocent young man stepped my foot from my silent life on the ruin piled up with corpses, I sensed only what a disaster has been undergone, but did not understand life very much. However returning to Tangshan, I suddenly felt I have understood something…

I seemed for the first time to survey my nationality, my compatriots, and my planet from an angle of disaster. This is cruel, however brand new. Such astonishing miserable change, such severe catastrophe, such tremendous dead and sorrow, by which I can not deliberate in a regular way; including all those things which are so beautiful that make man grieve; those which are so hard that make man tremble.

This is my Tangshan.

I spent the Spring Festival of 1985 in Tangshan, Aunt Lu Guilan who has been buried in the ruin for thirteen days ten years ago and invited me to make dumplings at the eve of the Festival. This lonely old woman, who has lost her husband and lovable daughter, treated me as her only relative. Her calling me "Child" once and again made me heart ache. The banging sounds of firecrackers outside the room shook my heart tremble. After the noon the shooting of firecrackers became louder and louder as to the evening it has been so close that one could not separate them from one another and the sky was shone to red through! I saw those youngsters, on the tall buildings, at the Road crosses light the string of firecrackers, fireworks, flash firecrackers, "chrysanthemum firecrackers", "silver dragon jetting pearls", "five presenting flowers"… but no laughter was heard. They remained letting off and off. I felt those deafening noise of bluster sipped extremely complicated feeling.

Doubtlessly the 240,000 people are a collection as a whole, which took away the perfect vigor and felling ten years ago and left Tangshan sensation of incomplete both physically and mentally. All seemed disappeared, all seemed to remain; as if to be no longer grieve; as if to be non-sorrowful sorrow.

Just all these impel to write down my Tangshan with my pen. I would like to leave anthropologists, sociologists, seismologists, medical scientists, psychologists of today and tomorrow, not only them but the human being on the earth a true record about the catastrophe, leaving the historical fact not having been appreciated; leaving too, to my deliberation and query.

This is my mind.

CHAPTER I

FALLING DAY JULY 28TH

. 3 o'clock 42 minutes 53 second

History will remember this coordinate of the earth forever: 118.2 east longitude, 39.6 north latitude.

The mankind will remember this moment on history forever: 3 o'clock 42 minutes 53 second July 28th, 1976 A.D.

Only one second earlier the surface of the earth seemed quiet at 118.2 longitude E, 39.6 latitude N., Tangshan of Hebei province of the People' Republic of China. Everything was silent as an ordinary day. It was late night everything was silent. Almost no man could be seen in the streets. On the wellhead of Tangshan mine Kailuan Mining Bureau, the head wheel was rotating at a normal speed; in the newly built seven-storied Kailuan General Hospital, several rays of quiet soft light penetrated the windows. The whole city was sleeping in silence. In the dormitory of some offices, a school girl named Jiang Chunhong was just going to her bed after spraying some DDT to expel mosquito; one staff named Lu Yanling of Hebei Mining College, worrying about the rain was collecting her clothing shone outside the window; a waitress Zhang Keying of the railway station was discussing their purchasing of the night meal with one of her colleagues; a doctor named Liu Xun was putting on his coat and was going out of his room for an emergency call…

Nobody has been informed, for some years the earth's crust under Tangshan has been changing horribly. In Tangshan and west part of Tangshan the magma and the hot material of the earth's up curtain and low earth crust was moving to the up earth crust speedily, forming a vertical force. A tremendous elastic stress energy made by the long time concentration of the strong crust stress produced by the move of the crust was accumulating string in the rocks. The rocks have been supporting themselves painfully till the disastrous moment when the strength of them was broken up suddenly. At 3 o'clock 42 minutes July 28th the rocks under Tangshan collapsed abruptly! They broke up!

At 3 o'clock 42 minute 53.8 second they burst abruptly as 400 atomic bombs exploded on Hiroshima in the earth crust 16 km deep from the surface of the earth.

It lightened and thundered in the sky above Tangshan, the wind howled on the ground. In severe shaking this city with a population of one million leveled to the ground in one second.

The vast land of North China shook fiercely.

Loud noise was produced by the falling of houses in Tianjin, the former Australia premier Whitelam being visiting the city was awaken, horribly flaws had appeared in the walls of the hotel where he inhabited.

Beijing shook constantly. The Monument of the People's Heroes was trembling; the gross beams and pillars on the rostrum of Tainanmen constructed with bricks and wooden creaked and cracked, as if to break up. On the vast land of great China, north to Harbin, south to the line between Bangbu of Anhui province and Qingjiang in Jiangsu province, west to the line between Chengko in Inner Mongolia and Wuzhong in Ninxia Islamic Autonomous Region, east to the island in Bohai bay and the national border of northeast, the people on this vast areas sensed this uneven shake. However the strong seismic waves had spread themselves throughout the earth in the way and at the speed unimaginable by man.

Alarming bell went suddenly at the Parmo Astronomical Observation, Alaska, and USA. Four seismologists and two technicians who lived in a fixed distances of five minutes speeding away hurried up to observe their instruments. They found when the alarm bell went Alaska jumped up and down in a scope of 1/8 inch, The inhabitants of Alaska called them one after another to require, "What has happened? Earthquake? Is that an Earthquake in China? Will grand earthquake happen in the United States"?

All the seismic stations over the world sensed the lashing power from China. Although not having been informed by the exact information where the center was, all the seismologists recognized that a tremendous disaster had happened. All the large news agencies over the world issued the results recorded by the various seismic stations on the day.

The US national seismological intelligence center said, "An earthquake of 8.2 magnitude has happened at 39.6 N., 118.1 E about 100 miles southwest from Beijing, near Tianjin.

The Japanese meteorology ministry said an earthquake of magnitudes 7.5 to 8.2 has shaken China, the center of which was at Inner Mongolia, i.e. 43N. 115E..

The Nagano seismic station, Japan declared an earthquake of 7.5 magnitudes has taken place in China.

The Sweden Uppsala seismology institute said an earthquake of 8.2 magnitudes has shaken China.

The inventor of Richter Ms. Richter (USA) declared that an earthquake of magnitude 8.2 has taken place in China.

The British Royal Astronomical Observations in Hong Kong declared the earthquake has taken place in China has a magnitude about 8, the center of which was at 118.2 E., 39.6 N., very close to Tangshan.   6

The central meteorology Bureau of Taibei, China said the seismic instruments at the saddle of The Yinyangshan Mountain has detected a strong earthquake in northern part of China, having a magnitude of 8, the center of which was 135 km east to Beijing. The total shaking time recorded by Taibei was about 1 hour 32 minutes.

Rays after ray's electric waves penetrated the space constantly.

However nobody could imagine that such a miserable situation had happened: in Tangshan a city of China with a population of 1 million has been leveled to the ground by the partial shake of the earth.

The New China News Agency issued the following news on July 28th: New China News Agency, July 28th, 1976: A strong earthquake took place at 3 o'clock 42 minute on July 28th, 1976 in the area of Tangshan, Fengnan in Jidong region (east part of Hebei province) of Hebei province of our country. Tianjin, Beijing had strong shake too. According to the measurement of our seismic station network, the magnitude of the earthquake was 7.5.

A few days later China republished the revised magnitude of the earthquake to Ms 7.8.

This was a disaster as puzzle.

The puzzling 3 o'clock 42 minutes. However in what way did all these begin with?

. Having Been Warned By Nature

It seemed to be an unforgettable unavoidable catastrophe.

But the nature had really warned. If at that time there had been a giant who had been able to survey a sphere in a diameter of several hundred miles, observing the various scenes in the sky and under the ground, he would have been sure to be surprised to those abrupt inconceivable changing phenomena of nature, even having a fashion of magic. It was those warns by the nature that made the seismologists when recalling, collecting them after the disaster have their hairs stand on their ends and to deliberate.

However to July 28th all these foresights were too late.

. The Extremely Horrified Fish

. The couple of Wang Baocang and Zhou E teachers of No. 8 Middle School of Tangshan;

In the middle ten days of July 1976, the fish sellers in the streets of Tangshan increased suddenly. The couple was astonished, "it has been difficult to buy fresh fish for a long time. Why there is so much fish these days and the fish is cheap?"

" Where did you catch the fish?"

"From the Dohe River reservoir," the fish seller told them, "it is strange that the fish is easy to catch these days."

The couple never thought of that a disaster was falling. A few days later, they lost both their daughter and son in the disaster.

. Chen Yucheng, a miner of Zhaogezhuang Coal Mine, Tangshan:

"On July 24th, the golden fish in his fish jars strived to jump out of the surface of the water, even out of the jar, the fish screamed."

. Huo Shanhua of the fishery of the fourth branch of Baigezhuang Farm, Tangshan:

"On July 25th, there was gurgling noise of water in the fishery pool, those grass carps jumped in groups, some jumped to a height of one feet above the water surface. There was more astonishing

Thing, some fish rotated like tops with their tails up to the sky and heads down to the surface of the water.

The Flies and Birds Losing Their Intelligence

The sailors of the oil tanker Changhu (Long Lake) on the sea at Dagukou, Tianjin, south to Tangshan:

"The sailors witnessed on July 25th the air above the sea around the oil tanker whistled, a large swarm of dark green dragonflies flew to us, dwelled on the windows of the tanker, also on the mask, lanterns and the buck densely, not moving, not flying up in spite of man's seizing anyway.

"Not long later a big disturbance occurred above the tanker, a large swarm of butterflies of all the colors; brown colored locusts, black cicadas as well as many mole crickets, sparrows and unknown birds flew to us, as it was an unexpected refugee party; the last comer was a tiger-skin

carrot in brilliant colors, who stood on the stern stubbornly, motionlessly.

Li Yinfu a teacher of Tangshan Mineral and Metallurgy College:

"On July 27th, taking part in summer harvest in Zhengzhuangzi commune in the suburb of Tangshan he saw the civil military battalion commander of Xiaodaizhuang village brigade had a string of bats in his hand in a number of more than ten, strung with a piece of thread. He said to him "Release them, they are of beneficial animals". The battalion commander said," It is strange these bats flew about in the yard in the day time."

Zhang You of Pingcun Town, Qianan County in Tangshan district:

"On July 27th, the old swallow under the eaves carried their youngsters in their bills flying away.

(At the same time in the home of a commune member in Xitangzhuang Brigade, Panzhuang Commune, Ninhe county south to Tangshan. The old swallows under the eaves of the house carried their two youngsters away: it was said since July 27th, this old swallow seemed to get mad, throwing her youngster out of the nest, no sooner the householder picked up and put them back to the nest than the old one threw them out again.

The commune members of Wangshizhuang, Banqiao, Ninhe County;

"On July 27th, the commune members working in the cotton field informed that a large swarm of dragonflies constructed a square formation, flying northward from south.

Flying and Immigration of Animals

Wang Gaishan of Wangdongzhuang village, Bencheng commune, Luannan County, Tangshan Region;

"On July 27th he saw by his very eyes that groups of mice were running about in the cotton fields, among them the older ones carried the youngsters. Those small ones biting the tail of their front ones to form a string. Someone felt strange, chasing to beat them, "Don't beat them. I am afraid there will be a flood. These mice are frightened to be drown." Someone of tender hearted persuaded those beaters.

Xu Chunxiang and others of Xuanzhuang village, Fentuo commune, Funin County;

"In the afternoon of July 25th, they saw more than one hundred yellow weasels, those big ones carrying small ones, or having them in the mouths, squeezing out of a hole in an old wall, fleeing the village. When it was getting dark, ten of them ran about under a walnut tree, five of whom were beaten to death at the very moment, the others screamed instantly, having horrified sensation of facing death. In the two days of 26th and 27th, this group of yellow weasels continued to immigrate out of the village in the air of surprising and frightening.

Those acute flies, birds, big and small animals marched their first step of fleeing much earlier than human beings. However man did not recognize that these were warning by the nature. They never thought that a tremendous bloodsucking disaster was confronting.

Those Unimaginable Signals

The Nature Really Warned Man

Along the coast southeast to Tangshan, the waves produced stirring and touching noise. Since the last ten days of July the fishermen of Beidaihe area were puzzling, "Why those reeves who were out of the surface of water formerly were drowned under the water now?" "Why was the coast on which only one stretch of net could be shone available for two or three net shone"? Those sea areas where they often fished became deeper than before. The fishermen almost distrusted their own eyes, the seawater of the sea area from Caojiapu to Dashentang closer to Tangshan always remained clean, why did it turn to yellowish muddy? It seemed that in the depth of the uneven sea, a dragon in tale was turning its tail, stirring the mud on the deep bottom of the sea.

It was said a diver who was in the seawater near Qinhuangdao at the time saw a colorful light band as a golden-fire-dragon disappear immediately. The water, the water was also warning man.

A motor-pumped well as deep as 50 meters in Yangguanlin commune, Fengren county, Tangshan Region gave off steam out of its cover made of concrete since the middle ten days of July. The spraying of steam reached its summit on July 25th, the noise of which could be heard 20 li from it (20 li=10km) and small lump of stone could float right above the hole of the spurting steam vapor.

There was another magic well in Gaokan commune, Luannan County, Tangshan Region. The well was not deep at all, a shoulder pole can be used to hoist the water from it in ordinary days; but on July 27th, a man found unexpectedly that the bucket hung on the should pole could no longer touch the water, returning home to get a piece of rope, the falling water rose up unexpectedly abruptly, not only the shoulder pole was necessary, the bucket in the hand could carry bucketful water. In those few days, in some villages around Tangshan, in some places the water in the pool dried up magically; in other places steam of water like Baotu Spring in Jinan spurted water pillar up in some pools. Water, the abrupt rising and falling of water, what signal was it transmitting to Man?

People sometimes received the signals from nature, however these signals were unimaginable.

On the top of the Foyeding Mountain, Yanqing county, Beijing Region as a height of 1,350 meters above sea level, 200 km from Tangshan there was a rainfall gauging radar; there was too a guarding radar of air force nearby. On 26th and 27th both radars received a strange finger like echo in the shape of fan coming from the sky of Beijing, Tianjin and Tangshan. This kind of echo was different from those jamming of sea waves, the disturbance flow of fine sky; or echo risen by birds, and astonished the monitors. When on earth such a wonderful magnetic field appeared in the areas of Beijing, Tianjin and Tangshan?

People were walking through such a strong magnetic field unconsciously.

On July 27th several soldiers in the barracks north to Tangshan shouted astonishingly. They found a pile of steel bars on the ground spurted flash inconceivably, as if a hidden man was doing electric welding there. (No man at all in fact)

In Beijing, Tangshan in the midnight many fluorescent lamps of the inhabitants kept lightening after being turned off.

In Tongxian County someone found a disassembled fluorescent lamp of 20 watts was flashing.

July 27th was an in conceivable day.

In the mining area of Linxi coalmine, Tangshan, a light yellowish fog floated, giving off a smell of sculpture. It blockaded man's sight and made man puzzle. People were fumigated to be confused, they could not see clearly the fact of the world, and could not make it clearer what a tragedy the nature was brewing.

If all these information had been collected, concentrated, transmitted and processed, perhaps the description of the disaster would have been another result. What was regretful was that the opportunity was missed. People, blinking their puzzled eyes, blurred and dimmed came to the late night of July 27th unconsciously.

Late Night of July 27th Before the Catastrophe

. Wang Cai of Caoying Brigade, Liyuan commune, Tangshan.
Having seen the film and going home at 12 o'clock in the late night I saw four ducks not be able to be herded into the yard but standing outside the door. Seeing their householder they cried in one voice, stretching their necks, swinging their wings, spreading their feathers, draggling up to him. They ran after Wang CAI wherever he went, biting the bottom of his pants desperately.
. Zhang Baogui of Dongdahu Brigade, Luannan County.
I could not fall asleep in the late night of July 27th. Hearing the cry of the cat, he thought the cat might be hungry and got up to feed it. The cat did not have anything, keeping crying and running about. (At the same time Wang Huihe of Liyuan commune, Tangshan saw by his very eyes that a female cat raised by his second uncle scratched its householder in the mosquito net, boldly to wake up him)

In that night people heard shrill bark of dogs for a long time in the area of a diameter of a few hundred kilos around Tangshan.
. Li Xiaoshen, a villager of Daangezhuang village, Yingezhuang commune, Tangshan.
The wolfhound he fed did not allow his owner to go to bed that night. Li Xiaoshen kept the door open when he went to bed. When the dog could not wake him up, it bit him fiercely. He jumped up because of pain, running after and beating the faithful wolfhound.
.Su Yumin of Zhouyuan Brigade, Xianghe County;
The bitch of Su's had her three puppies born on July 21st in her mouth one by another to the empty ground, she even dug a hole to put the puppies in it.
The night got late and late, this was a noisy night. July 28th was coming in this uneasy atmosphere.
At 1:30, Zhang Chunzhu of Dashantou marten farm, Funing County was awakening by the squeaking of the martens. The 415 martens of the farm scampered, jumping and knocking in the steel nests extremely horrified.
Simultaneously, the broiler farm in Suguantun Brigade, Baiguantun commune, Fengren County was in disturbance; about 1,000 heads of broilers ran fro and back in disorder, jumping on the windowsills, crying noisily. The farmers fed them however the broilers had no appetite at all, becoming more and more uneasy, as if to be pursued by something, about one or two hundred broilers swung their wings, flying about in the nests.

At the same time Chen Fenggang was getting up to feed his horse in a cart inn, who was of Guta Brigade, Zuojiawu commune, finding the horses and mules knock and bite each other in disorder, not be able to stop by loud urging. At the time over three o'clock, all the horses of more than one hundred of the sixty carts broke their reins, loudly neighing, bouncing out of the horse shed one by another, bolting on the highway wildly.

Simultaneously Li Huicheng of Matiezhuang Brigade, Jiangqiao commune, Changli county, Tangshan Region witnessed by his very eyes more than 200 pigeons of his neighbor flew out of their nests abruptly, flying above the roof, wheeling about, knocking to each other, not landing for a long time.

The horrible moment was coming up and up.

A few commune members of Angezhuang village, Luanxian County jumped out of the pool with screaming. The water of the pool was pumped from a hot water well nearby, the temperature of which was 48 to 49 degrees centigrade in ordinary days. The few young men doing night work jumped into the pool to bath. The water was too hot to withstand. They were puzzled and cursing. Never had they thought that the quake of the earth was approaching.

It was approaching. The commune members looking after the melons of Changli county saw the sky 200 meters above the ground turn bright suddenly, shining the ground to be white, the leaves and vines of the melons could be seen clearly, "Why? Is it getting dawn?" A middle school student of Fengren County felt the same; rubbing his sleeping eyes, he saw it bright outside the window. The leaves of the cucumbers shone in bright white light. Watching his watch it was only over three o'clock a.m. being astonished, it was getting dark again, so dark as to be dyed by black ink.

At the moment the earth was in silence ahead of the catastrophe.

Apparently many people had received the warning signals by the nature before the Tangshan earthquake. However these warning signals were of "not-to-be-sole". The hot weather could drive the broilers and dogs uneasy; the continuous rain would raise the water in the well. People explained these uneven things with their even experience.

A humorous photo was carried by the "Earthquake Information Bulletin" published by American Geological Investigation Agency in 1978, a chimpanzee horrified to close his eyes and open his mouth; remarks were written, "Why I can forecast the earthquake while the seismologists can not!"

This was the self-criticism of human. However people often forget, "Man is the animal of society. Even in the struggle with nature, man can display his force as a whole; when man fights lonely he has not much advantage over animals. Relying on his instinct man is even much backward than animals. Confronting such a tremendous and magic natural disaster as earthquake, man has not constructed a complete alliance, having no respective communicating ways and methods to process and collect the unexpected signals of nature timely. How couldn't they be beaten one by one by the devil falling abruptly?

Remember the Warning by Nature Forever!

The Words of Those Eyewitnesses

To leave the offspring true historical information, I looked for them once again and again. It is true that the disaster happened in the overwhelmingly silent night, the witnesses seeing the process of the earthquake were extremely rare. This writer shifted the audio record of the nine investigated people as reference to all.

Li Hongyi (A nurse of former infectious department of No. 255 Hospital PLA)

"I was on duty in latter part of the night that day. Before midnight it was both humid and hot. I could not fall asleep at all. Being on duty after 12 o'clock p.m. I was very sleepy. Staying in the wards up to 3 o'clock, I went out to take cool under a big tree. I remembered that I was sitting beside a mall stone table used for playing chess formerly.

"The surrounding was quite quiet. I felt strange very much because at this moment of an ordinary day, there would be chirping of insects, crying of frogs noisily. What on earth was it today? There was not any voice and sound at all, too quiet unexpectedly, so quiet that horrified people.

"Suddenly I heard a strange creaking flying over my head, of wind? No. It was not like the crying of an animal either. I could not make it clear what it was like and could not to compare with others. I have never heard such cry before. The voice was sharp and shrill, like a knife cutting across the sky. I was trembling and had goose flesh all over."

"Rising my head to look at the sky, it was cloudy where there was a piece of cloud of strange shape. It was neither in red or purple. The curtain of the sky was very dark. I thought, "Is it going to rain? Lifting my foot to go to the room.

However I was flustered magically, which I had never had previously, as if someone was pursuing to fetch me. I was bold generally, daring to stay in the mortuary lonely. But I was frightened at this time, with heart beating violently, walking and running, but not be able to run fast in my slippers.

Turning my head to have a look, I saw the sky in the northwest extremely bright, like to be on fire, but no one calling for help. Everything seemed dying. I became more and more frightened, fleeing to the room, turning on the light at once and bolting the door.

At this moment I heard the big bang of zooming, like hundreds of trucks to be started, "Damn it!" I had heard such noise in Cangzhou when the Xingtai Earthquake occurred. I deliberated immediately, "It is the earthquake."

"As thinking, the house rocked fiercely. The thermal bottles on the table fell down to the ground and crashed. I exerted myself to open the door and could only open half of it. I dashed out of the room to a big tree.

"I put my arms around the big tree tightly. In darkness I felt the earth was shaking and swaying, both the tree and I were falling, falling and falling in a valet of thousands of feet. There was no noise in the surrounding. I could not hear the noise of the houses' falling at all. Only the shadow of my dormitory building could be seen a moment ago disappeared now."

"I stretched my hands in front of my eyes but could not see anything. I was frightened to be foolish and roared desperately, "Ouch…""

Tian Yuan (A peasant of Daodi Brigade in the suburb of Tangshan)

"Hey, the night was really terrible."

"I was threshing crops outside the house when the earthquake occurred. Why did I work so late? It had been raining for days. The wheat in the threshing yard would be muffled to decay. I could do nothing but did extra shift.

We finished the job up to three o'clock. Someone went home after collecting the tools, the other two and I stayed to clean the threshing yard.

"Suddenly, like beaten by thunder, it was booming. The earth shook fiercely and the mountain rocked. I fell down to the ground as to be kicked by a sweep led, turning to the left first and then to the right, unable to stand up. The lights in the threshing yard were off at once.

Cocking my head, my God! It was horrible, a large fire ball went out of the ground, which was red through and dazzlingly bright, creaking and cracking, being off after flying in the sky.
When it got dawn I saw a flaw in the ground where the fireball went out, the soil aside was burned.

Jiang Dianwei (a veteran worker in Kailuan Printing Factory)

I was exercising Taijiquan (a kind of Chinese martial arts) in front of the gate of Fenghuanshan (The Phoenix Hill) Park when the earthquake took place.
I suffered from high blood pressure and was taking sick leave. I learned a set of 24 forms (one type of Taijiquan) from an old man over seventy who got up at three every day. As one of his fellow students I die the same. In the morning on July 28th, we met at the gate of the park at three thirty, together with us there was another man named Tang.

We chatted for a few minutes before we were ready to do the exercises. We heard the noise of booming like fierce wind blowing, also like the steam whistling in our coal mine in the old society. I was facing southwest, while the old man to northeast. I heard his crying, "Damn it! It is on fire." Turning my head there was a stretch of red   in northeast.

Not having been reacted the ground began to rock. It rocked first and then swayed. The man named Tang held the fence of iron bars of the park tightly. The old man and I, standing with our legs apart, held each other tightly. We talked at the beginning and I said, "The earth shakes and mountains rock, those beggars put down their begging bowls. There should be a bump harvest next year." The old man said," No, it was on fire." I said, "No, it was earthquake."

Quarreling for a few words, there was rocking similar to that in a big sieve, like being sieved fiercely.

Cracking and banging the boundary wall fell down, followed by the crashing of the buildings opposite in one moment of blinking. The debris and rubbles of bricks and tiles were cracking, dust flying about, and the sky fouling up. "Damn it." I said, "Hurry up to home to dig up man."

My home was not far from the park right aside the railway. I was made a fool, not being able to find my way home when I ran to the railway. Oh! The stretch of houses around my home fell down all over.

Yang Songting (an officer from the department of construction of Tangshan Gas Company)

Before the earthquake occurred it was hot and suffocating, having a sensation of fogging. I was sixteen years old that year and have not got a job yet. I was offering a hand as an assistant in the safeguarding group of the policemen of the branch security of Lubei District, seizing the thieves and those fleeing criminals. In the evening of July 27th we were on patrol duty in the area of long distance bus station because it was crowded and in disorder. Over three o'clock on 28th, finishing our work we fellow brothers were sitting and chatting in front of the hotel of the bus station. Suddenly the ground under our foot shook. There was also roaring as those oxen, also like the sound heard at the wind gap. We were frightened to jump up, running to the center of the street. The road was narrow. We were afraid to be buried by the falling houses or pounded by the falling lanterns, which collapsed with one blow.

I put my arms around a fellow named Wang Guoqing. However we could not support ourselves as a pair of hands was separating us apart. Both of us fell down to the ground. Standing up by effort, joined by the third man, tried we three to support ourselves to stand but failed. We seemed standing on the deck of a ship on the top of waves, swaying as the ship swayed. We held each other tightly. The ground was still rocking by which we felt that we were having pins and nails in our feet.

Just at this moment we heard the "bang" noise of the falling and collapsing of the houses, smelling the choking of the dust. Crowds of people ran to the streets, nobody could run fast, swaying, rocking, with one fall to each step. I saw three female peddlers fled their sales sheds. But the woman cooking jellied bean curd of the station restaurant did not escape, being pounded by something; her head was dashed into the boiling pan.

Song Baogen (a switcher of Tangshan Railway Station)

I was almost shaken to fall down to the ground to death from the carriage by the earthquake. I was a switcher. Before the earthquake occurred I was hitching the carriage on the special line. All right it was loaded with bamboos and was piled up very high, on which I sat to wave the signal lantern. Displaying the driver a "March" signal, he went the steam whistle and started the

Locomotive. I heard a loud noise of banging. The carriage began to shake. The first mind came to

Me was, "Damn it, it was derailed." Displaying a "stop" signal, however without finishing my waving I fell down. It was rocking fiercely. Tossed from the top of the bamboo pile, I rolled to the carriage side," God bless me. "I held the iron wire bundling up the bamboos, not fearing the wire cut into my flesh, unhitching meant death. There was rock once again; fortunately it was not rocking side to side but back and fro. I had my hairs upside if it rocked side to side, the carriage was sure to overthrow.

As soon as the rocking stopped I slipped down the carriage. The front lamp of the engine was on. Seeing forward, my god! The pen-straight railway twisted to a shape as fried dough twist, zigzag as a long snake. I, at this moment saw that it was earthquake and heard someone shouting," hold the railway, the earth is sinking."

I dashed to the ground at once, holding the railway tightly and was frightened to be a fool.

Zhang Keying (an attendant of Tangshan Railway Station)

I never forgot the banging of the earthquake for my lifetime. I was frightened out of my wit.

I got up over 2 o'clock to be on duty that day, selling the platform tickets in the inquiry office. About over three o'clock, someone was shouting, " It will rain. It will rain." Hurrying out of the office to bring my newly bought bicycle. I saw the sky glooming. It seemed there was lightening somewhere. The people on the station square rushed to the waiting hall to take shelter.

 At the time, there were about 200 people in the waiting hall, of whom there were men to meet passenger, wait-for-getting-boarders, also those who got down the train, waiting for the first bus. In a noisy air I heard two young people, a man and a woman asked me for two platform tickets for meeting someone from Beijing. I said,   "There is no train now. Come for your tickets at five." The couple did not leave, standing at the window to wait. Who on earth knew that what they met with was the earthquake?

Before the earthquake occurred, I was talking with master Chen, separated by the glass of the window, discussing our buying the night meal, asking him to bring me two steamed stuffed buns. Not having finished m words I heard the banging. What a banging. We were shaken to be puzzle. I thought that two running trains at high speed crashed each other. Without shouting all the lights in the waiting hall were off, where became pitch dark. The building began to rock and great disorder happened in the waiting hall. There was so much noise of calling Dad and Mum, people stepped on people, something knocking another. The flopping and thumping were heard first, of which the pendent lamps and fans fell down on the heads of the people. Those pounded children and adults shrilled miserably. A moment later, the station hall broke up. It was more than two hundred people who were tamped under it.

   Thanks to the door leaned on the shelves of the left luggage office, which placed me in between, I was not fatally wounded, hearing two crying near me, "Ouch, ouch." "Mum."

I could not recognize that they were the man and woman waiting for the platform tickets, who cried once without the second voice…"

Liu Xun (the vice-section-chief of the medical affair department of Tangshan No. 1 Hospital)

At three thirty in the early morning of July 28th, I was in a sound sleep, hearing someone knocking my door, "Doctor Liu, Dr. Liu." in an extremely anxious voice. Opening the door to have a look I saw it was Wang Kaizhi of the suburb hospital. He said,   "The patient to have been operated on by you and I was in danger. Would you mind to have a look?" This night call was really of coincidence.

No sooner I put on my clothing, stepping out of the threshold together with Mr. Wang Kaizhi than there came the earthquake. It swayed first with the sky wheeling and the earth rolling, swaying so fierce that we could not stand, unable to walk on either, followed by rocking. Our feet seemed to be electric shocked by the rocking. Continuously the debris and rubbles of bricks and tiles fell down. It was strange that we did not feel pain when this debris pounded on our bodies and only felt flustered. The booming of the earthquake was too terrible. I have seen the documentary film of volcanic eruption; there seemed a pan of molten iron in the crater. At the moment of the earthquake I felt more frightened than that standing at the crater. Man cannot control himself at all; rhythm of heart was out of order entirely. It was pitch dark and dusty in the surrounding. The houses collapsed and fell down to the ground.

A moment later man could run abruptly. I myself wondered when I did begin to run. However running for three or four steps, I felt it was wrong under my feet. Looking at them, how could I get on the roof.

Zhang Zunqing (a worker of Tangshan Power Plant)

When the earthquake occurred, I was on duty in the controlling room of the boiler. Suddenly the building began to shake, the readings of all the meters became irregular. For only one second, the whole set of equipment were off automatically. The plant turned to pitch dark.

I felt down to the ground. In the controlling room the chairs were overthrown, the thermal bottles were crashed, the safe helmets, tool bags, flashlights fell down to the ground with cracking. Seizing a flashlight in my hand, I immediately did the process of separating the water and steam of the boiler. Nobody knew what had happened, only recognizing that the most serious accident has happened to the electric wire net, which should be recovered immediately.

Rushing out of the controlling room, I heard the cracking and creaking of the building, the pounding of the bricks and saw that smoke was reversed from the extinguished no. 8 and no. 9 boilers. We were surrounded by the boiling hot smoke and dust. There came the shouting through the black smoke, "It is earthquake now." The chief monitor on duty ordered everyone stuck on his post, that who leaves his post privately will be brought to a lawsuit."

The air of the plant was tightened to blasting point. The houses were falling and the ground was shaking. The puzzling alarm bell tooted, together with the electric bell, small trumpet, noising madly. The most frightened sound was the exhausting sound produced by the several boilers, the safety valves of which were playing their parts, the steam of the boilers, in a pressure of 100kg per square cm spayed out fiercely, producing the ear-piercing shrill. All the people were astonished to be bold by their thrill, which was louder than the exhaust by more than 100 locomotives, as if to tear the hearts of the people to pieces.

. The Dying Morning

Tangshan missed her dawn for the first time.
She was covered by fog of dust all over the sky.

Limestone ash, soil, debris of coal, smoke and dust as well those materials of death produced by the destroy of a city mixed the gray smog. The dense smog spread, floated; in pieces, rays and mass rose, as a curtain floating in the sky gently, silently covering the ruins, and covering this deadly quiet city.

All the sounds and voices disappeared, occasionally, there came the weak crying of children, which too, like transmitted from great depth of the earth, which was so sound and lonely, so long and thin, like a piece of white thread going to break in hallucination.

All the voices muted; this smog of death hid all the lives. In the misty smog, the former Tangshan could no longer be seen. The following situation of several scenes of Tangshan were witnessed by my very eyes or referred to the information,

The ground floor of the four storied book storage building of the library of Tangshan Mineral and Metallurgy College made of reinforced concrete structure slid westward, the former four storied building seemed to be swallowed one story by the earth crust, cutting short of her height.
. In the Railway Station, the rails of the east part turned to a shape of curve as a snake. Having a bird view, it looked like a flat calabash made of steel rails.
. The seven storied Kailuan Hospital became a triangle slant tomb like tower; on the top of which only the structure as big as two rooms remained, which put itself up with slant and tottering gesture on the debris falling wall.
All the balconies fell, the one of the second floor pounded vertically on that of the first in its falling but not falling down.
. A piece of wall in the dormitory building of the party committee of the city was overthrown completely, the side of the second floor of which exposed six pieces of space where all the family apparatus were exposed, as the tables, beds, even a small table lamp.
. In the foreign guest hotel under the foot of Fenghuangshan (The Phoenix Hill) the two storied restaurant only had its infrastructure remained, on the ruin wall of which the elegant wall lamp could be seen outside.
. The concrete road in Tangshan No. 10 Middle School was broken across, half of which turned to left, the other half to right, the dislocation of which was over one meter.

The trees along the Jixiang Road seemed to flee the earthquake at the moment, some of which tried to "run away", and have left the line of the trees, but "were pulled back", the dislocation between the trees and line was over 1.5 meters.
The most astonishing thing was in the area where the earth flaw of the earthquake passed, as the party school of Tangshan district party committee, the Dongxinjie Primary School, the agriculture institute of the district, as well the whole Lunan inhabitant district, which seemed to be bolted by a gigantic hand. Imaginably, there seemed a black devil wreaked havoc there, it was he who leveled the streets and lanes, broke the bridges, pitched off chimneys, overthrew the train out of rail. A prank of nature changed the face of Tangshan thoroughly. Those scattered concrete beams and pillars, those old machines wreckage, those slant electric poles, those half water towers, inclined east and west, laid or were oblique, like those sculptures in a vast piece of mass grave.
In the dense smog there was no groan, no shouting, there were only those mechanic steps of men, those heavy breaths, those deliberating and anxious conversation as well as the higher and higher piles of corpses! Those heads squashed, those feet smashed, those body flattened.
A concrete beam spiked a female soldier through her chest.
A lying-in woman who was about to give birth died, blood flew out of her lower body.

An opened novel "Sword" pounded a lovely child's head when he died, but he could never reopen his book…

Doubtlessly this was the most miserable page of human history. Those innocent dead people, almost all at the unprepared condition were put to death abruptly. It was too hurry, too quickly; the death was of one moment.

 In the dismal smog, the most trembling thing was those corpses hung on the ruined buildings, one of which had his hand compressed by the slab of the building, head lowered; someone was pounded on the feet, the whole body hang in the air upside down. They were the most acute group among the victims, awaking from sleep, having got out of their beds, running to the balcony of or in front of the window, however their retreating path was blocked by the devil of death. A young mother had stretched half of her head of the window of the second floor, but was pounded on the windowsill by the heavy slab. She died in the midair, child in her arm, defending the young life instinctively at the moment of death, following the shake of aftershock the hanging hair of this mother stroked in the fog.

 Has there been such instance that a city was destroyed in one morning in the history of China? The Shaanxi earthquake in 1556, the Gansu earthquake in 1920 did not occurred in the densely populated city. In spite of this the heavy death and wounded shocked the world. However today Tangshan beaten by the earthquake of Ms 7.8 is a city populated with more than one million people.

 It was a vast stretch of ruins.

In Xiaoshan of Lunan district, an old woman luckily fleeing the disaster struggled out of the ruin. Everything in front of her furled her mouth, unable to say anything. Where were the old streets? These were old streets of long history, these consistent prosperous old streets. Where were they? Where was the Dashijie (the Grand World, a commercial center at the time) Where was the Laoziyuan? (Theater where Ping Opera was performed) Where were those vaudeville theaters? Where were those bathhouses and pharmacies? Where were those shops selling Qizishaobin (sesame cake with pork pie inside in the size of a piece of Chinese chess) Kaipingmahua (fried dough twist made in Kaiping, a town near Tangshan) and Tangshan roast chicken? Where else those old sister with whom she went shopping, basket in hands? Where have they gone? There was a stretch of deadly silence. There was neither road nor path at all. Only by those standing electric poles could she recognize the old streets. The streets were narrow formerly the old buildings at either side of it fell upon and filled them. Those getting-up-early sanitation workers, the cart transportation soil were buried in the narrow old streets The more miserable was the area of those one storied houses, along the lanes these houses were trampled flat with one blow by the devil, as trampling a pile of egg shells.

 At this moment the area changed into an empty and amazing square, where ill wind was blowing chilly, several shadows of people were standing on it dully.

Tangshan people were standing, on those ruins covered by the dense smog; on the roadsides covered by the dense smog; they stood, stood boldly. Many of them were still in dream, was it the blast of atomic bomb? Was it an accident of the coalmine? They didn't know to clean the blood flowing on their faces, didn't know where they were staying. In nonsense someone held a dead goose in his hand, did not loose his hand anyway. Someone staring at the dead child in the foot basin did not move at all. Many people were stark naked, those girls only in their bras, forgot to find a clothing to cover their bodies. Tangshan people named Lushi described those survivors he saw in the dawn in the memory after the earthquake.

Because most of them crawling out of the ruin naked, they covered their bodies with everything available. A considerable part of them were in pajamas of foreign style, which had broad sleeves and long tot heir feet. I knew that these were products for export purpose, fetched by the victims from a nearby tailor's factory; several young men wore gray uniforms and caps of New Fourth Army of old China, two of them wore the caps of Japanese soldiers, another was in Japanese riding breeches. All these were costumes of one modern Beijing Opera named "Shajiabang". A white beard old man having a stick in hand and up body naked, wore a flowered skirt of young girl on his lower body. A teenager boy came up arm in arm with a mid-aged man, who had his leg wounded and limp, putting his hand on the shoulder of the boy. His right hand held tightly a sword in a fish skin sheath, the bright orange tassel dangled gently beside his leg. Perhaps the sword was handed down from his ancestor…

The colorful crowd dangled in the gray fog, still frightened, dragging like a group of sleepwalkers. All of their organs were paralyzed; their lachrymal glands, their vocal cords their nerves transferring pain were paralyzed. They were stubborn, senseless, even did not grieve in time for the departure with their blood relatives.

The sun rose, like a piece of round thin and light paper cut, it slipped in this densest, dying fog. Its flaming hot light burned the dense fog thinner and thinner, starting to float. Tangshan in faint would awake. When the fog scattered up, the horrified people found two wolves fleeing the zoo, in the same fear. Leaning to each other, they stood on the faraway black ruin, opening their horrified eyes lonely, breathing in uneasily fear. Suddenly they bounced up as if to be frightened again, start to run faster and faster, jumping over those broken walls, those collapsed roofs, those piles and piles of corpses, running around the Fenghuangshan Hill like arrows, as if to seek a living path. In puzzle they two ran to the top of the Hill, stopped at last in the gesture of the stone carvings. Facing the whole broken Tangshan, facing this boundless stretch of ruins, they roared shrilly, much like the cries of Tangshan people.

In the morning of July 28th, this remaining fog and roar of wolves did not scatter for a long time, not scatter for a long time.

A pile of information of the earthquake and photos taken at the top of Fenghuangshan Hill was put in front of me.

The Great Wall was as the northern border of this stretch of ruins; the beacon tower has fallen down;

The tower of Liao Dynasty locating in Jixian county has flaws in its body, the top of which has fallen down to the ground.

The East Tomb of Qing Dynasty locating in Zunhua county were the graveyard of 161 Empires, empresses, imperial concubines, princes and princesses including empress Cixi, the carved stone man and stone beast of which were overthrown by the earthquake.

Only in these few seconds the ancient building condensing the history of thousands of years received the sound shake from the crust of the earth.

Beside my ears, in front of my eyes, the roaring of wolves and the dense fog in the morning on July 28th reappeared. I imagined if there had been a historian facing this stretch of ruin at the time, what would he has seen?

Tangshan did not have a long history as a city. It was nothing but a small town in the Ming Dynasty. However the abundant resources underground seemed to make it sure to have her way of incessant stream of horses and carts. People dug coal, cast stones, and manufactured potteries here. The villages became closer and closer, merchants and traders concentrated here. She was established as Tangshan Town in 1878, the name Tangshan was given after the existence of the stone castle at the northern part of the city, which was built in the Tang Dynasty when Empire Taizong (one of the famous empire of Tang Dynasty) on his way of his eastern conquer (another saying was there was the grave yard of General Jiang Xing of the late tang Dynasty) Tangshan is a city where modern capitalist industry has been developed Rapidly. Both the first self-built railway and the first self made locomotive in the history of China were produced in Tangshan. (The railway is from Xugezhuang to Tangshan and the locomotive was named Longzihao) How about nowadays? The historical Tangshan No. 1 middle school, which was built not long after the Reform Movement in 1898, was destroyed at the very morning together with those middle schools and colleges established after the 1950s. In the display room of "Potteries and Porcelain Made in the Recent 500 Years" of Tangshan Porcelain and Pottery Company, the jars and basins of ancient and modern exported porcelains; thin fetus porcelains, fine bone porcelains, tea sets, table wares, drinking vessels, smoking sets, coffee sets turned into fragments together with the falling of the slabs of the building.

Looking back to the human history the brilliant civilization of Indian River drainage area continued for more than one thousand years, the center of which began to decline by the time of earthquake high tide era in the eighteenth century B.C. Today some foreign scholars concluded that the earthquake caused the decline of the ancient civilized cities in the drainage of the Indian River and floods occurred 1,700 B.C. ago. 1,600 years before the century, the Crete Island in Greece suffered from earthquake of Ms 10 degrees three times; as a result this pre-history vast civilized area disappeared. Crete culture was destroyed.

Then what about today's Tangshan?

If there had been an architect standing beside the historian, I think his sight would not have been faraway, but of reality.

He would have seen that the most severe earthquake area of intensity 11 degrees located at the area of Tangshan city, starting east from Yuehe Commune in the suburb, west to the storage of Tangshan local products company and Hebei Mineral and Metallurgical College, south to the Nvzhizhai commune, north to the line along the Coal Mining Institute and No. 21 Middle School. The isoseismic line formed an ellipse shape, the major axis of which is as long as 11.8 kilos, while the minor axis is 3.5 to 5.5 kilos, the area dimension is 47 sq. km.

The following is the conditions in the area of intensity 10. Starting east from Guye, Dazhuangtuo commune, west to Langaozhuang commune, south to Daodi town of Fengnan County and Donggezhuang commune, north to Fujiatun commune and Wangnianzhuang commune, the area dimension is about 320 sq. km.

The following is the conditions in the area of intensity 9. Starting east from Buozhuang of Luanxian County, south to Xiaoji, Fengtuo, Xigezhuang, Lizhuangzi of Fengnan County, the area dimension is about 1430 sq. km.

The following is the conditions in the area of intensity 8. Starting east from Shimen of Lulong County, west to Lintingkou of Baodi County, north to Huoshiying of the northern part of Fengren County, south to the Coast of Bohai Sea, the area dimension is about 5470 sq. km. (the destructing degree in Tianjin has reached intensity 8)

The area of intensity 7

Starting east from Maguying, Zaoyuan of Funin county, west to Qigezhuang of Dachang county, Bieguzhuang of Yongqing county, Dafengtan of Jianhai county, south to Qikou of Huanghua county, north to Sanhe, Jixian counties and northern part from Zunhua county, the area is about 26,000 sq. km.

In the most severe damaged area, most of the industrial buildings collapsed and destructed, the roofs of which fell down in large area. The enclosing brick walls, especially those external brick walls, the supports between pillars changed their shapes fiercely; the reinforced concrete pillars had flaws, smashed or broken. The destruction of multiple storied plant buildings were more severe. As to all the civil housings those multiple storied brick lime structured collapsed entirely. The bricks used in many new buildings were of poor quality, almost similar to handmade bricks, all of which smashed to debris to the size of a fist after rocking. The falling of the brick walls, the collapse of the roofs of the houses, the breaking of the slabs of buildings wounded and killed people mercilessly.

As to the housing in rural areas, the major part were built with bricks and stone, bearing the weight of roofs which were made of coal cinder and lime stone ash. Houses of this structure were severely destructed in the area of 8 to 9 intensity areas, fell down in large scale in the 10 degrees area, and almost collapsed to the ground entirely in the most affected area. The reason of falling or collapsing was that the walls were low in strength, the roofs were too heavy, and the jointing and junction were loose.   17

Housing is originally the shelters where humankind protects them, preventing from rain and wind. In the history of development man has managed from living in caves to learn to build houses, from building houses with grass and wood to constructing buildings of bricks, stones or metal. The inhabiting shelters have been improved and evolved continuously. But in the grand earthquake people were killed directly by the falling of their houses. The housing doubled the disaster and became the accessories in assisting the tyrant to do the devil, becoming the tombs of the people.

Of the total number of civil houses of 682,267 rooms in the rural and urban areas in Tangshan (10,932,272 square meters) 656,136 rooms, a floor space of 10,501, 056 square meters collapsed or destructed severely in the earthquake.
 All these were really astonishing. Tangshan is an area where no destructive earthquake had been recorded before, the urban architecture did not protect from the earthquake, the protecting degrees of which was only 6 degrees of intensity. However it was right here the earthquake of magnitude 7.8 and intensity 11 degrees occurred.

Apparently the expert sight of architects would stare at some other buildings. In the area of 10 degrees of intensity, the entire superstructure of an eight-storied building is still standing. This is the unfinished Xinhua hotel. The former design of this building was inner-super structured while the external bearing weight. After the Haicheng earthquake 12 structure pillars were annexed to the external weight bearing walls. As a result the building withstood the earthquake and did not fall down. Also those houses simple in section, with smaller doors or windows, light in weight to both wall and roofs survived from the disaster.

Facing the cruel fact that several hundreds thousands of people died of those fragile building, how much sorrowful deliberation and critical pity would these surviving houses cause those architects to think of?

I thought, too. If, at the moment, there had been an economist who had bird-viewed the ruins of Tangshan, what a list of figure s being silent but astonishing he would have read?

Tangshan, the renowned industrial city in northern China, the area dimension of which only makes up one ten thousandth of the country, the population makes one thousandth, but her output value makes up one hundredth of the GNP of the country.

Tangshan has been known as "the capital of coal". Taking Kailuan Coal Mine, the largest throughout the country, she has constructed her own heavy industrial system. The coal output of Kailuan Mine made up one twentieth of that of the nation, playing a part as pulling one hair would affect the whole body of the economic life of the country. Her coal varieties took burden coal of coke-making, rich coal as major part; in addition to supply Anshan Iron and Steel Company, the Capital, Benxi, Baotou Iron and Steel Companies, the civil utilization in Beijing, Tianjin and Shanghai areas, also exported to Japan and Korea.

The electricity industry in Tangshan holds the balance. The Dohe River Power Plant built in 1976 is the major power plant in northern China electrified wire netting, as well the largest thermal power plant of our country. Tangshan is as well, the famous "Huabei Cidu"(the porcelain capital in north China). Tangshan's porcelain and pottery can compete with those of Jingdezhen, her total output value of ceramic industry from the founding of the nation to 1975 surpassed one billion Chinese yuan (RMB)

She has also metallurgy, textile, cement, motor vehicle, machine building, she has many very important enterprises.

However today almost not a single chimney could be seen in the whole city, this largest industrial city in Hebei province.

As a tremendous economic living body Tangshan had no longer breath, no pulse no flowing blood at all at this moment.

In only a few seconds this extremely important pillar of the national economy structure of China was smashed mercilessly.

A kind of strong economic shaking wave would spread over north China and whole China. Was there a more terrible fact than that a fatal important energy basis was destroyed?

The countable direct loss of Tangshan's economy in July 28th earthquake reached the figure more than 3 billion Chinese yuan (RMB).
The cost in rescuing the disaster and rebuilding the city is almost uncountable.

On March 4th, 1835, the great evolutionist Darwin arrived at Conception city in Chile where fierce earthquake just happened, facing a stretch of ruins he sighed in heavy emotion... "The achievement that human realized by countless time and work was destroyed in one minute; however my sympathy to those refugees seemed to be lighter to another sensation, that was, the amazing feeling caused by the changed situation that deserved several centuries to be realized generally, but has realized in one minute..."

So was the sensation of countless Chinese to Tangshan Falling Day, July 28th.

Chapter II

Tangshan- Hiroshima

In both domestic and abroad, to both today as well ancient time many military scientists often linked the grand scene to a destroying earthquake when they described the war.
However those generals undergoing hundreds of battles and fights, when conducting bird's eye view to the ruins of Tangshan in helicopters in commanding disaster relief at the front said to me,   "This earthquake is much like a unprecedented cruel war."

"I have never seen such tremendous number of deaths and wounded people, never seen much miserable scene..." Yang Lifu, the first grade disabled soldier, the vice commander of the logistic department of Beijing Military Region said, "In the first few days arriving at Tangshan, I had evil dreams every night, in each of them I dreamed Hiroshima the catastrophe of which I have seen in the military documentary film. The atomic bomb destroyed a city, debris and rubbles spread over the land everywhere, people were burned into inscribable appearance... but the damage in Tangshan was much more severe than that in Hiroshima. Several hundreds thousands of people died in a single morning."

Tangshan-Hiroshima were two falling cities, one of which could be taken on war launched by fascists, taken out on man themselves who launched the disaster to human society; but what about this time? The seismologists said the energy of the seismic waves released by Tangshan earthquake of MS 7.8 is equivalent to the total amount of energy of 400 Hiroshima atomic bombs (however the energy of seismic waves only make up few hundreds of the total amount of energy of the earthquake)

"The Red Ambulance

At about 4 o'clock ten in the early morning on July 28th, no more than thirty minutes after the earthquake, a red ambulance was driven out of the gate of Kailuan Coal Mine with booming. Rolling over the debris and rubbles it ran into the Xinhua Road, rocking and swaying in the vast gray fog, it dashed westward at top speed. This was the first post-earthquake walking vehicle in Tangshan in which four men were taken.

These four men never thought that at the time only three hours later their red ambulance would appear in front of Zhongnanhai in Beijing and they three would step in the meeting room of the vice premiers of the state council.

History would record the names of these four men in the ambulance: Li Yulin, the former vice chairman of the trade union of Tangshan Coal Mine, Kailuan; Cao Guocheng, a staff of the military department of Tangshan Coal Mine, Kailuan; Cui Zhilian, driver of the mine ambulance corps of Tangshan Coal Mine; Yuan Qingwu, winch driver of the machinery power department of Tangshan Coal Mine.

All was decided in a moment.

When they crawled out of the ruins of their dormitory district in Zengshengli, the first mind came to Cao Guocheng and Li Yulin was "Go to report to the party committee of the Coal Mine!" Ten minutes later they saw the piles of debris of the office building of the party committee of Kailuan Mining Bureau, as well the party committee of Tangshan city turned into a stretch of ruins too.

Simultaneously Cui Zhilian on duty at the mouth of airshaft thinking an accident happened in the airshaft drove a car to report the emergency.

The four assembled had no time to discuss or consider, the disordered frightened feeling, anxiousness and astonishment concentrated into one short words out of Li Yulin's mouth,   " Get aboard, look for a telephone."

"Yulin, let's go to the party committee of Tangshan Region!" Cao Guocheng shouted.

No sooner than their leaving the gate they saw GAO Jinhua, the vice director or the public security department of the mine run up. Li Yulin cried, "We are going to call up and go wherever we can, you should organize to defend the mine…"

The red ambulance dashed along the Xinhua road. Opening his eyes astonishingly, Li Yulin saw seven big guest hotels along the road turned into ruins. He counted carefully only several tens of people were standing along the road. This was Tangshan.

"Where was the party committee of the region?"

"Where was the military sub-area?"

Xiao Cui, the driver said to Li Yuling, "Uncle Li, I listen to you and go wherever you order me."

"Westward, westward." Li Yulin said.

Shouting for help spread faintly out of the ruins. Someone blocked the way by waiving their hands, asking to transport the wounded people.

"Don't stop." Li Yulin forced himself to be ruthless. "Hurry up! It is more important to call up."

Large plums of brick flew to the ambulance, the men along the road were cursing and damning.

The way of the ambulance was blocked again in the suburb of Tangshan. There were crowds of people, wounded, corpses as well as cement poles lying in the center of the road…

"Send these wounded to Tangshan, Send these wounded to Tangshan as soon as possible…"

"Hey! Tangshan has been leveled." Cao Guocheng popped his head out. The houses fell down, where are those hospitals? Hurry up to organize self-relief."

"This is the car to send message!" Li Yulin jumped down the ambulance and shouted,   'Time is the most valuable thing. The earlier the authorities know the news, the more lives will be rescued.'"

The crowd began to move; they removed the corpses aside, shifting the stones away, moving away the cement pole traversing the road. The car crossed the bloodstained road.

Fifty miles per hour, sixty miles, and seventy mile… one piece of broken wall after another dashed over the window fast; one ruin village after another blew on. Li Yulin, this former soldier of the Chinese People's Volunteers, the motorcyclist of the First Games of PLA was a heavy built, over bold man. In the high-output-movement days, he had worked for eight shifts day and night without break; in the mining accident he often exerted himself to the very site.

At the moment, with his up body naked, only in swimming trunk, stared at the road with flaws ahead. Cao Guocheng in shirt waved his miner's helmet outside the window, once and again signaling the walkers to give the way. Cui Zhiliang had his hands holding the steering wheel, trembling slightly.

The front place was Yutian County.

The courtyard of the party committee of the county was there.

The secretary of the party committee of the county carrying his pistol on his shoulder was walking about the ruins.

Telephone! Where on earth was the telephone?

One authority of the county committee blocked the way of Cao Guocheng and others, asking countless questions. He asked what unit they were of, what their social vocations were, what their political background were, followed by the questions about the situation in the courtyard of the Region party committee. (People knew later his family habited in the courtyard)

The red ambulance continued his trip on the road. Telephone; there was no telephone available. What about front? Was there any expectation in the Jixian county ahead?

When a string of blocked Cao Guocheng "no" said by the Jixian county committee, he was worried almost to blast his head. "Hurry up! Hurry up to go!"

But three men of the State Seismology Bureau rushed out, they were looking for the center of the earthquake and just arrived at Jixian county.

"Are you from Tangshan. Be better hurry; hurry telling us the situation there… Alas… alas… You'd better send one comrade return to Tangshan with us, while we send one to follow you…"

The ambulance went on. Yuan Qingwu got on the car of the seismic team, returning to Tangshan. A comrade named Bian of the seismic team jumped into the ambulance. Hurry up. Hurry up. Hurry up to find the telephone. It was not until they arrived at Tongxian County in the suburb of Beijing, Li Yulin and Cao Guocheng did not give up calling up Beijing in a factory. The old doorkeeper said, "What on earth do you call? You will be there by your car before the call is up."

All right! To Beijing!

This was another decision made in a second. Li Yulin and others, staring getting their nerves tightened since 3 o'clock 42 minutes suddenly found their ambulance had arrived at the entrance

of Beijing on their way looking for a telephone.

Sounding its alarm the red ambulance rushed in Jianguomen of Beijing, speeding like wind and lightening, dashing along the rained broad road, being regardless whether red or green lantern.

" Let's go to the Seismic Bureau!" Lao Bian said.

" How long will you take to report to the central party committee?"

" Collecting information will take half day…"

" Half of a day? Would it be more troublesome than that of a call?" Li Yulin almost shouted, " To the State Council!"

The red ambulance dashed to Xinhuamen.

During my call to Li Yulin, the sick-leaving cadre of Tangshan Coal Mine and Cao Guocheng, the director of the service company of the mine, I noticed they were still keeping the special experience stamping in their brain.

Ten years have passed great changes have taken place on the political stage of China; many hurry passengers have been forgotten. However the uneven historical event would be retrieved. What was important to Li Yulin, Cao Guocheng and Cui Zhiliang was not the men they met that day, but was their existence itself, was what they did for the several hundred thousands dying people.

I am responsible to write down their memory.

Li Yulin:

… A police blocked the ambulance ten meters from Xinhuamen. The guarding soldier ran up as soon as Xiao Cui stopped the ambulance. With my up body naked, I jumped down the car. The police asked, "What are you?"

I said, "I came from Tangshan to give the alarm to the State Council."

The attitude of the police was kind, he said, "Go to the reception Center of the State Council. It is at No. 4 Fuyou Road, turn to your right as Liubukou."

Arriving at the gate of the reception center, putting on a ragged garage uniform and coming in, I saw my hands were bleeding, which were shed by the mother whose child was raked out by me after the earthquake. Squatting on the roadside washing my hands and face with rainwater, I went in.

It was eight o'clock six minute in the morning.

As officer of PLA was in the reception center, hearing alarm reporter from Tangshan, he entered to call up immediately. Soon later he went out and required us to fill in the form. Just them two comrades of the air force arrived by plane from the Tangshan airfield.

The comrades of the air force and we were shown the way to Zhongnanhai. When entering, a Hongqi (Red Flag) car was coming out, brushing us.

At that time the emergency meeting about the earthquake was ascertained initially. The No. 1 party secretary of Hebei Province Liu Zihou and Xiao Han, the minister of the Coal Ministry were ordered to go to Tangshan by airplane immediately. The two air force officers entering Zhongnanhai together with Li Yulin and others were Liu Huran, the vice political instructor of some air force regiment and the latter, Zhang Xianren, a staff of the division office. Taking the Li-2 airplane piloted by Guo Yongfa flight crew of Lanzhou air force carrying out a task to Tangshan, they took off at 6:51 and landed Beijing at 7:40.

Cao Guocheng:

We were shown the way to Ziguange in Zhongnanhai. There were several vice premiers at the moment. Li Xiannian, Chen Xilian, Ji Dengkui. There was also a large map spreading on the desk. With red pencils in hands they pointed here and there in a tight air. A minute later Wu De came in, the several men asked in one voice, "Lao Wu, what about the suburb of Beijing." "About 400 houses fell down in Tongxian County."

Seeing our entering they stood up. I said, "Your honors, Tangshan was leveled." One of the officials I forgot his name said to us, "There. There. Don't worry. Sit down, have a cup of water, tell slowly…"

All the men asked in voice, "What about the situation?"

Crying as I spoke, "Your Honor. Among the one million people, at least 800,000 are being buried in the ruins."

All men cried.

Li Xiannian asked me, "How many people are there in the pits?"

I said," Ten thousand."

"These ten thousand miners are in danger…" Li Xiannian asked again, "Which are more? The buildings or one storied houses in Tangshan?"

I said, "There are more buildings in Lubei District while more one storied houses in Lunan district. The two kinds are almost in balance."

"We'd better rescue people as soon as possible."

Chen Xilian handed over a piece of paper and asked me to draw a sketch about Tangshan. Wu De came up to ask, "Where in the location of the building of the General Administration Department of Kailuan built by the British?"

Pointing to the sketch, I said, "Here it is. It has collapsed."

Wu De sighed. He has been the party secretary of Tangshan and knew the old building built by the British was so solid, the wall of which was as thick as one meter. Wu De said, "Tangshan did not exist, Tangshan did not exist."

Cao Guocheng:

We claimed the followings, "Send armies, send mine ambulance teams, and send medical teams."

It was really posthaste at the time. Our claims were discussed one by one in the meeting. The several vice-premiers stood up and then sat down. Someone asked Chen Xilian immediately, "Lao Chen, which troop was near Tangshan?" Chen Xilian reported a list of designations and where they stationed of the field armies. Just at the moment, one PLA man came in to report, Li Desheng, the commander of Shenyan Military Region is ready to set off. The comrades of the air force accompanying us opened their bags and fetched out the maps, pointing out the locations of the airfields over the nation, helping to schedule the program of getting aboard of the ambulance teams.

There was a sketch of nervous voices in the meeting room.

"Call the General Staff Office to send someone here!"

"Call the Air Force to send someone here!"

" Notice the authorities of the Public Health Ministry, Commercial Ministry, the State General Material and Goods Bureau to come here for meeting immediately."

" The Coal Ministry, also the Coal Ministry. Where is Xiao Han?"

" He went to the air field with Liu Zihou…"

" Oh, that's all right. Tell him to stay in Tangshan and no need to return. Call the vice minister of the Coal Industry Ministry."

"He'll be here a moment later or he's on his way here."

It was possible that Ji Dengkui who presided the meeting, comrade Li Xiannian sat aside. Lowering his head, Ji Dengkui sometimes turned his head back and asked him,   "Would it be alright, comrade Xiannian?" Comrade Li Xiannian put forward his opinion and gave an appearance of heavy hearted and looked older than his age.

Half of an hour after our meeting, some PLA men sent us few sets of their uniforms and some army doctors came to check up us. We almost exhausted at the time, while Mr. Yulin was to vomit.

The authorities of the various ministries of the State Council arrived. They held an emergency meeting. We were shown the way to the neighboring room to have some meal, beef cooked in soybean sauce, salty-duck-eggs and small steamed twist rolls of weighing only 15 grams each. We were so hungry but could not eat anything. Someone came in and said, "You've done your job." We were so exited that we did not know what to say, only shouting, "Long Live Chairman Mao."

The coming of Cao Guocheng, Li Yulin and Cui Zhiliang awaked the vice premiers of the State Council to realized profoundly the seriousness and the scale of the disaster. The nation was disturbed.

At ten o'clock Xiao Xuanjin, the vice commander; Wan Haifeng, the vice political instructor; Zheng Xiwen, the vice director of the political department of Beijing Military Region; Liu Zihou, Ma Li, the party secretaries of Hebei province; Ma Hui, the commander of the provincial military command; Xiao Han, the minister of the Coal Industry Ministry landed.

At 2 p.m., three planes carrying the commanding officers of Shenyang Military Region, as well the medical teams of Liaoning province landed.

From 4 o'clock p.m., five planes carrying the ambulance teams from Datong, Yangquan,

Fengfeng, Fushun, Zibo, Huainan coalmines reached Tangshan respectively.

At the same time the relief troops were marching forward Tangshan in two ways of southwest and northeast; the medical teams throughout the country were being organized rapidly…

In the morning of August 1st, 1976, at Hongqiao Airport, Shanghai; the relating authorities did not agree with my getting aboard the plane flying Tangshan, a Trident fully loaded with plastic film bags to contain corpses…

"No, no, we can not communicate with Tangshan now. You will not be able to find the Shanghai medical team by yourself."

"It does not matter, I shall manage myself."

"That will be dangerous, there is neither meal nor drink, and there are infection diseases everywhere…"

"I should go to collect news there."

"Go with the epidemic prevention team by train"

… I arrived at Tangshan with the epidemic prevention team.

I began collecting materials about Tangshan…

Dohe River Dohe River

The Dohe River Reservoir was in emergency.

This was an unexpected emergency. After the earthquake, the dam of the Dohe River Reservoir locating 15 km northeast to Tangshan sunk one meter downward. The major dam broke as long as 1,700 meter along lengthwise; there were also transverse flaws every 50 meters, having a total number of more than 50 flaws. Some of the flaws were as wide as one meter, as long as eleven meters. It was raining heavily. The water level was rising rapidly. The dam was in imminent danger. The bottom of the reservoir is ten meters higher than the ground of Tangshan city and the total storage of water was 36 million cubic meters.

Provided that the dam collapsed, the lake of water over the head of Tangshan people would dash down with roaring and would drown the earthquake struck Tangshan, which would be a miserable situation.

Dreadful, unimaginable secondary disaster!

Was it a historical instance that Tokyo was destroyed by the fire followed the earthquake in 1923?

"Hurry up!"

" The dam of the Dohe River Reservoir would burst!"

"The water is flowing down!"

In the tempest those earthquake survivors camping around the reservoir were in great disorder, crying and shouting, not taking in account to bury the corpses of their relatives, not managing to unbury their valuable materials and goods. Carrying their packs and children in arms, only could they run to the high slopes as far as their legs could carry them.

The horrified sentiment spread over rapidly and formed dangerous situation at once, endangering the public feeling.

The situation was really in emergency; the booming thunder mixed with the roaring of waves in the reservoir could be heard clearly.

A troop of soldiers was running towards the dam of the reservoir. They were the soldiers and officers of some artillery regiment stationed near the reservoir, just fleeing the ruins they received the order to protect the dam. The regiment headquarters sent soldiers to the dam first, to prevent the dam from destruction by the "class enemies". But they recognized the emergency of the situation soon later. In the tempest, the rapid rising water was roaring as boiling, those steams were misty; the muddy waves lapped with booming, the dam was full of flaws. It was the situation that black clouds presses the city to collapse.

At this time the flood of the upstream of the Dohe River was dashing down like wild horses, the water level of the reservoir was rising terribly, where there were whirlpools, mad waves and the dam with flaws. People might be able hearing the moan of the dam under the great pressure of the flood, but no longer to withstand it. The reservoir was saturated, while the water entering it was increasing without limit. The broad and thick dam seemed to be as thin as a piece of transparent paper; the danger of its collapse was on the verge!

It must be spilled and pressure reduced, which was the most key link over all.

Dong Zunsheng, vice-chief staff of the artillery regiment leading the soldiers of the eighth battery rushed up the dam for relief, he shouted loudly, "Open the spillway gate!"

However the power had been off for a long time.

The switching machine of the gate could not be started.

He led the soldiers rushing into the winching room to lift the two gates as weight as 40 tons by the hand winch.

This was a moving and amazing scene, the soldiers in groups of four revolved the winch by the force of their arms, which was as weight as more than one hundred thousand jin (1 jin= 1/2 kg)

The wind was blowing and the rain was pouring, the earth remained shaking in the aftershock; the devil waves were still shining in the lightening, the sound of the waves was as loud as thunder with foams flying about. From morning to the night the creaking and cracking of the hand winch spread out of the cabin, as well the work song sung by the soldiers in nervousness and tire.

It was extremely difficult. Four strong young men lifted the gate less than one centimeter by turning one hundred cycles, seven or eight hours passed, the soldiers kept working in shifts, as if saving time with their lives.

The spill gate was hoisted in one millimeter and another. The dam survived, the reservoir survived. The secondary disaster after the earthquake was avoided.

Standing on the dam of the Dohe River reservoir, I gazed the white water in the distance. It was in winter of dry season, but in front of my eyes there was still water linking the sky, the tides were roaring and the waves piling up; I could not help thinking what a scene would it be when the mountain like torrent rushed down.

On my way driving to the artillery regiment, I felt the car was going up and up. Doubtless on July 28th of the year, if the Dohe River Reservoir's dam had burst, where I passed would have been a stretch of ocean.

Wei Shide, vice battalion commander as a squad leader at the time took part in securing the dam. He showed me the uneven winch room locating above the spillway, upon which there was the huge spill gate. It was difficult to imagine why this "temple in the air" did not fall down that day. If so the soldiers in the cabin would have not only been killed, but also fell to the valley as deep as several meters. Wei Shide and his comrades-in-arms did not know this great danger at the time.

Wei Shide;

We became really scared when thinking about the situation that day.

We thought it easy to lift the gate at the beginning, thought it would be lifted by several work songs, who on earth thought of it took seven and eight hours!

The winch room was shaken with many flaws. Standing outside the room one could see men inside; the room would collapse at any time. We had dug up those dead people in the early morning, with blood on our bodies. We knew what it was to be pounded.

Everyone attending was anxious and nervous. Revolve, revolve the winch desperately; pearls of sweat fell down with click, with heart went pit-and –pat. Each group worked for ten minutes, changing shifts as soon as possible. In those ten minutes, anyone was possible to lose his life, but no one shrank.

There was a stretch of crying and shouting, over which those refugees ran in crowds. Our guarding post shouted loudly to persuade the people leaving the winch cabin, which would fall any time, passing rapidly the dam with flaws.

At the time we thought the dam would collapse any time.

After ten minutes work we ran away from the dam and squat on the slope. However when anyone was in his shift, they ran up without any words. I thought at the time, how terrible would it be if the dame collapsed? Tangshan would have had a secondary disaster after the former!

We were just like in a war, marching forward meant death, so did retreat, we exerted ourselves…

With arms naked in those trunks, we turned the winch desperately; with hands and skin worn, almost waist broken; we kept shifting in every ten minutes first, but broke it afterwards, the working hours became longer and longer, even the shout to shift could not be heard!

In the evening there came a strong aftershock, by which the dam cracked and boomed; the winch room rocked fiercely, the people outside of which slid down to the ground. I was outside the room at the moment with heavy palpitation. I lay on the ground and thought there came an end, the dam would destruct, the winch room would fall down! But the dreadful thing did not happen. The dam survived, the cabin survived, there also spread the work song of my comrade-in-arms…

I never forgot the situation that day. By night the two spill gates were lifted at last. We heard the water gurgling through the spillway. Being relaxed, we felt exhausted and became limp to the ground…

Avoiding the secondary disaster after the July 28th earthquake in Tangshan would not be said to be unfortunate. Apart from the dam of the Dohe River, there were also two other places where encountered danger at the time, one of which was Kaiping Chemical Works. The earthquake destructed the valves in the liquid chloride workshop. The dense poisonous liquid chloride leaked and two people were poisoned to death immediately. Because of timely relief, also because of heavy rain diluted the toxicant, no severer damage occurred. If so all the tens of tons of liquid chloride had spilled, it would have threatened all the refugee camps in Kaiping area. The second was the gasoline deposit in Gaogezhunag petroleum store near Tangshan Iron and Steel Company, the gasoline tank was broken by the earthquake, more than 1,300 tons of gasoline in which flew about the ground. A spark would cause a blazing prairie fire. By the timely guarding by the army, the fire was avoided. It happened that those heroic soldiers guarding the oil deposit just belonged to the artillery regiment who took part in relief to the Dohe River Reservoir.

Kailuan Coal Mine! Kailuan Coal Mine!

In the morning of July 28th no one doubted the most miserable sufferers in the disaster were those ten thousand miners in the pits.

At the beginning of the quake, they were left underground in the depth ruthlessly.

Unable to run the steaming whistle, but it was more than terrible to any alarm steaming whistle. Those women crawling out of the ruins not caring to clean up the blood on their bodies, calling the names of their husbands, running to the gate of the pits with hair standing on the end. There was crying, shouting, the disordered crowd resembling a gas explosion having occurred, the roof fall occurred, the water penetrating occurred. No, no other accident could match the miserable situation of the day. Almost all the buildings on the ground fell down, what about underground? What about those thin tunnels supported by those round woods? Those working sites where were full of danger in ordinary days and what about those vertical shafts? Those inclined shafts?

Guo Biao, vice director of Kailuan Mining Bureau ran to the dispatching office with one step deep and another shallow. His house broke but did not fall down, and he was the earliest escapee among the authorities of the bureau. He dared not to see all happened in front of his eyes, nor did he imagine the situation in the pits. In the night of 27th the whole Kailuan Mine carried out a High-Yield production activity, most of the officials and miners went down the pits. The slogan popular at the time was "Learn from Kailuan, Catch up with Kailuan." Those were ten thousand people, ten thousand people... The dispatcher's office had turned to a stretch of ruin, every mine had had power off and ventilation blocked. Guo Biao was rent with grief and at his wit's end. He never thought of that unbelievable fact that the underground equipment of various mines of Kailuan had not been destructed. Ten thousand officials and miners were striving to relief themselves, seeking every means to return to the ground by various ways.

Tangshan Coal Mine

The miners retreating the working areas concentrated in the major tunnel in a total number of more than 1,600 people. Three chargers of the three mining areas held an urgent mission and decided to lead all to retreat through the major tunnel of 15 lies (1 lid= 0.5km) and go up through the street of the second shaft of the mine. What so-called street was actually a thin inclined combat readiness path leading to the ground.

In the no. 13 tunnel without floating air, the troop of more than 1,300 people set off difficultly, the new workers of whom were at the front, the elder ones followed, those rank-and-files were ahead, those party members followed. They held their arms of each other and called gently...

Along the stretching line of thousand of meters, one seemed unable to see the shadow of man, but that string of moving points of lights, those one another lanterns resembled one another staring eyes...

Three points of light moved and rose in the pit as deep as 900 meters, moving and rising without yielding. No. 9 tunnel, No. 8, No. 7, No. 6... It seemed marching forward the land from the very deep bottom of the sea. Being dizzily, exhausted, they sensed the damp street endless. The No. 5 tunnel, people at last felt the cool wind in open air.

This was the natural wind sent by the ambulance team members by opening the ventilating gate. The wind sent them expectation...

Lvjiatuo Mine

More than 600 people, including 100 officials, several tens of women and few new miners taking part in the work for only 6 days, led by Jia Bangyou, the member of the standing party committee of the mine, having across the crisscross tunnels, came up to the reserve vertical shaft.

They should climb up the metal ladder as high as 100 meters!

"Hold to the ladder!"

"Do not release your hands!"

This was not different from climbing up a cliff of 100 meters along a scaling ladder. Those new miners were trembling at the gate of the shaft; those tiresome women having hands and foot weakened; someone was weeping. But the hands of some others held them powerfully. It might be said that a powerful strength pushed them up to the long ladder.

This was a troop going up vertically, a stream of lives floating to the gate of the shaft, going on so slowly, so difficultly, the bodies of flesh moved inch by inch sticking to the chilly cliff, with the fingers holding the ladder steps. Those women and young miners held by their downers and dragged by their uppers; in the nervous postures, climbing up step by step, as if following a strong up-going torrent of air, coming up to the ground, coming up to the ground.

Fangezhuang Mine

The working site of a new shaft was in a tight air. The cage stopped working, several tens of workers sinking the new shaft were blocked in the shaft as deep as 520 meters.

This large-scale vertical shaft called as "Pool of Dragon" poured from the bottom of the shaft and drenched more than 50 tons of water per hour. The workers were staying at the bottom of the shaft of more than 60 sq. meters and could be drown within only few hours.

A safety ladder slid down the shaft slowly, on which sat the vice-director, Guo Zhengxing of No. 1 mine construction district who was going down the shaft to organize relief. Holding the two strings of steel cables sticking to the wall of the shaft, he slid forward the valley by touching; perhaps when the workmen of Kailuan mine were striving to climb up to the ground, only this young man of 20 years old was matching downward the depth of the earth. The earth was rocking; the spray of water was splashing and flying. He kept touching and climbing in this pitch-dark shaft for three hours! Every minute of these three hours was struggle between life and death. He was cut sometimes in his hands by the steel cable, sometimes because of unable to touch the cable turned and hung in the middle air, in the most dangerous time, the safety ladder twisted with the steel cable tightly, he could neither went up nor down, untied the buttons in the darkness…

Finally he heard the voices of the sinking workers.

Since the duration of Li Hongzhang, the Northern Sea Minister and inspector of Zhili (the previous Hebei province) in Qing Dynasty in 1876, ordering to investigate the situation of coal and iron in Kaiping region to the time of grand earthquake in 1976, Kailuan coalmine has just a history of one Hundred years. In these one hundred years how much uneven experience has she undergone? The deceiving occupation by the British business men, the stationing of the Japanese Army, one after another strike and rebellion by the industrial workers…

Tangshan earthquake would write a new chapter in the one hundred years history of this mine,

When the severe natural disaster happened, the rocks and soil, combining into one piece entirely with the earth so that it was not prone to be destructed by the seismic power, blocked the appliances and equipments in the pit and shaft. Also the acceleration generated by the earthquake decreased as the depth increased, those structures in the pits and shafts were destructed less severe than those ground structures instead. Among those ten thousand miners and officials working in the pits, in the situation of power off, as well hoisting stopped, except 17 men who sacrificed on their post or missed their way to the mined area because of being unfamiliar to the tunnels, the several missed, the rest went up and retreated to the ground safely in the afternoon of July 28th.

This was really a wonder.

Of those people sacrificed heroically, I should write down the name of a rank-and-file worker, Zhang Yong. I heard his story ten years ago in Tangshan again and again. He was a storekeeper in charge of explosives and detonators. When the miners retreated to the ground, he had been able to escape from danger, but without the complete collection of the explosives, worrying about some accident might occur, he returned to the pit to look for the missed explosives till the rapid rising water swallowed him.

Destination: Tangshan

Tangshan

Tangshan

On the very day of July 28th, every highway leading to Tangshan was dust-flying –about and motors booming, one hundred thousand of relief troops of PLA were marching forward Tangshan day in and out. The transmitter receiver vehicles waving their antenna, transmitted signals to the troops constantly; countless Jiefang trucks carrying full load soldiers, blowing their hurry trumpets one by another, linking a long dragon on the muddy uneven roads. It was just like "in the early days of war". What they were encountering was a war, a war with mountains collapsed and ground broken, a war where corpses lying about the battlefield, a war between man and the nature.

Any soldier taking part in the earthquake relief at the time has not forgot the strong impression, a troop and troop of relief armies, looking like in the post-atom-blitz by the enemy, marching forward the destructed city at the fastest speed in hurry, disorder and anxiousness…

Southwest line: Gaobeidian-Tangsahn

Some motorized armies were marching forward Tangshan speedily. Gao Tianzheng, the vice political instructor at the time still remembered every thrilling moment from early morning to late night of the day after many years.

At 3 o'clock 42 minute the one another barracks rocked horribly in the shaking of the earth. The soldiers rushed out of their dormitories, the commanders of the battalion went to their commanding position immediately, communicating with their authorities to find out what had happened on hand, ordering the troops to be attitude of awaiting orders on the other hand.

At 9 o'clock, five hours after the occurring of Tangshan earthquake, the battalion received the order to set off to conduct relief to Tangshan as the advance troop whose armies were dispersing in 23 stations in 7 counties, whose circumference was more than 100 kilometers? Carrying out the tasks of training, building barracks and production, the front commanding head quarter of the army made the decision: set off as gathering (draw in) march forward as organizing into teams. Taking the combat readiness scheme moving to the district of Beijing, Tianjin and Tangshan as the bases, the fighting and training department of the division made the march plan rapidly, delivering the march map to every truck.

At 9:30, "the No.2 Red Company" of some regiment as the "Dagger Company" left their barrack.

At 10:20 GAO Tianzheng together with a vice-commander of the division led the advance regiment setting off.

For years they had nor undergone such exiting, moving scene. The black clouds filled the sky, like the pitch black smoke of gunpowder, the booming of thunder like shooting the guns, a batch and another bandaged were coming up in front of their eyes… It was Baxian County, Tianjin. There were street-filled sheds made of plastic film, street-filled people.

The relief armies passed one another cities, towns and villages in a stretch of moaning and crying, marching forward the center of the disaster. At about 4 o'clock the motorized army stopped marching suddenly. It was Ji canal, the bridge of which as long as 150 meters was broken at the waist part and fell down to the torrential waves. The troops were blocked on the south bank of the canal; all the commanders of various grades were worrying extremely, to build a boat bridge? It would take more than five or six hours, which were fatal five or six hours. They could see the blackish crowds of refugees, who were waving their hands and shouting. On this bank thousand upon thousand army men were blocked on their way, the soldiers were tamping their feet, twisting their fists. In the dense night the blazing vehicles lanterns could be seen everywhere; in the tempest the anxious calling of walkie-talkies could be heard everywhere…

Finding a tractor road finally leading to Tangshan passing Yutian and Fengren counties in the map, the political instructor of the advance regiment Luo Shengli put forward a suggestion to the front headquarter: change the marching route!

The armies blocked on the road almost turned their end to head, countless army vehicles turned their heads with great difficulty, roaring to dash on the thin and muddy tractor road.

In the late night the thin road kept rocking in the booming of the vehicles, the smell of gasoline and diesel oil was floating in the air above the field of a circumference of tens of kilometers.

The drivers had been rocked in their vehicles for more than ten hours. A motorcycle reporter to deliver orders back and fro, because of continuous marching had his legs burned to blister by the hot engine.

An exhausted driver picked from his pocket the prepared peppers constantly, chewing full of mouth to escape from sleeping.

A driver catching cold and having a fever more than 39*C disable to support himself asked the health worker to give him acupuncture. With the first treat failed, the second failed he required the health worker to leave the silver needle in his acupoint, every time his eyelids turned together, he asked the health worker to twist the needle, with the strong ache stimulating to refresh himself…

At 3 o'clock 40 minute of July 29th, just 24 hours after the earthquake, the advance regiment entered Tangshan.

The Northeast Route

Shanhaiguan-Tangshan

Some army of Shenyang Military Region was marching day and night.

The advance troop too, was blocked by the waves roaring river. The highway bridge had been broken, the only route of the vehicle was: force their way by passing the destructed railway bridge.

"I take my jeep leading"!" a commander of the division, pointing to the commanding jeep shouted, "I will die in my jeep if I must die!"

On another road, the battalion political instructor of the time never forgets the experience of the day. When the troops were carrying out firing practice in the morning, the authority delivered the order to set off at once to conduct relief to the disaster.

The officers and soldiers ran 10 kilometers to the barrack where the dinner was ready, but the whole troop got on the vehicles without carrying anything. The cooks put out the stoves by a ladle of water and set off with the troops with the pans on their backs.

On the bank of the Luanhe River the bridge of which had been broken, the tired and hungry soldiers and officers got off the vehicles, swimming across the river, marching forward on their feet.

The wet through army men walked speedily under the blazing sun. They were exhausted by a layer of suffocated steam, water dripping from their bodies, rain water first, and followed by sweat. They were seizing time with great efforts in the extremely hot waves.

The soldiers were tired and exhausted. They did not take a rest from early morning to night, keeping running, swimming across and force march. They did not have dinner, no supper and were starved to have sparks in their eyes. The most unbearable was thirsty, with which the throats

Burned soldiers were breathing with their mouth open, with the sweat pearls on their faces dripping and flowing down. They were extremely thirsty… three of them had been faint. Suddenly the troop were undulating, in front of them beside the railway, there was a stretch light, as if a pool of sewage water. The acute health worker immediately recognized, this was the wastewater drained by the train. Running to the political instructor Wang, he asked him to issue order "Do not drink the dirty water." "Every company pays attention no one is allowed to drink the dirty water."

Who on earth knew that this order got a contrary result; almost all the soldiers saw the light of water, like leaving the shooting gun, they swarmed forward the railway side. These deadly thirsty young men, bending their bodies over the ground of fragment stones, drank desperately the black water soaked with coal fragment and could not help from stopping whoever shouted.

It was getting dawn when the No.2 battalion arrived at Tangshan, the soldiers sat down powerlessly. The cook squad constructed the field kitchen at once, with which they boiled a pan of porridge… Fetching their mugs to stand up, the youngsters wanted to have a mug of hot porridge, but they sat down together without prior consultation; the porridge pan was surrounded by a group of hungry Tangshan children.

The first pan of porridge was shared to the children.

The second pan of porridge was offered to the kinsfolk beside the road.

Without third pan of porridge was ready, the soldiers received the order, dashing to the ruin…

It brooked no delay; in spite of their exhausted effort the relief troops were late. Tangshan had been moaning in the severe pain for a whole day.

The City in The Severe Pain

When the one hundred thousand relief troops were running on the highways, Tangshan was in convulsion, in pain and was reviving.

The post-quake blackish rain was pouring Tangshan as downpour, similar to the situation of many post-quake days in history, there was endless downpour. No one knew since what time a stretch and another stretch ruddy liquid began oozing out of the ruins of Tangshan. It seeped more and more, amassed more and more, like one another thin ruddy stream, flowing out of the flaws in the concrete cast, dripping along the twisted steel bars, winding the broken lattice of windows and frames of doors.

Seeping out of the gray white debris of walls people saw clearly at last, this was the blood shed by the bodies of those dead people buried in the ruins. The light red blooding water flew slowly getting together a ruddy river, leaving one another trace of lives that had passed away under the black ruin.

All the Tangshan people undergoing the disaster on July 28th were not able to forget this soul-stirring scene in the tempest, especially those who crawled out of the along this and another orbit were more unable to forget.

The Record of Interview (1)

Yao Cuiqing a workwoman of Tangshan Construction Bank, a girl of 23 years old at the time. Half of year ago she had been a pretty woman soldier, a female actress of an Army Propaganda Team. She stripped the uniform for only a few months, having a stable work just now, having fallen in love just. Her life seemed linking with songs, applause, smile and sweetness, but…

. I lay on the ruin moaning when reviving. I did not remember how our dormitory building fell down in rocking. I only remembered my companions around me were shouting. I thought it was a dream and awoke from it with extreme effort but failed. It was not until my mouth and nose were stuffed by dust, and body seemed to be blocked by the blade of a knife, still I thought it was an evil dream. I wondered too, how I was rescued, and by whom. I only remembered a bundle of heavy steps coming up from distance to nearby, and a voice of a man. With severe pain I fainted again. I never thought the pain came from my backbone, which had been broken. I could never stand up.

Lying there I fainted sometimes and awoke by pain a moment later. I felt the gray sky was low, as if weeping and sighing. I felt unbearable thirsty, "Dress… my dress…" I was lying naked. Someone threw me a pair of trousers, wondering whether because it was pants of child, or because my legs were swollen. I could put up only half of the pants. My legs had become paralyzed, as if they were no longer mine.

The scene of the time was very terrible. I saw a woman not far from me was spitting blood with mouthful, a boy was bending his body over a corpse, weeping. There was also a hair disheveled girl holding a dirty eggplant in her hand, swallowing.

I was extremely thirsty, stretching out my hands trying to get something, but I could say nothing only looking at the girl. Suddenly I found under the body of the girl there was a beach of blood, which was getting larger and larger.

The survived houses around were still falling down. Around me there were disordered crowd of men, among whom someone was shouting, "To the air field!" After a moment, my elder brother came; he carried me to a broken screen door, and loaded me with a wheelbarrow with the help of another man. I asked him where we were going. My brother said to the airfield. Wondering in what mentality that day, as well at the moment, almost all the Tangshan people placed their expectation to the airfield. As a result, on the highway as long as 9 km leading Tangshan city to the airfield, people poured forward it as tides. Noises disturbance fear, an unprecedented flees.

People never doubted that airfield was a place where the wounded could be healed and the dying people would be saved, a place where the hope of survive existed, all the people who could move fled there desperately. There were people who held tree branches in hands, carrying each other, naked, barefooted. It was said a middle aged woman refused to loose her hands in her arms when she cherished her dead kid; a middle aged man crawled along the road, clutching the stones on the ground, moving toward the airfield one inch by another. Some people only having their skin broken on head or bodies also joined into the fleeing crowd with a sentiment frightened out of their wits. This was a disordered, blooding road of surviving.

At ten o'clock it was raining again, the airfield was jammed by those wounded people and refugees, and becoming more and more miserable. There were wet through trembling people everywhere. The movable ones among them were searching for food and clothing everywhere.

Lying on the screen door, I was wet through by the heavy rain. I had been wounded so seriously that the medical unit in the airfield could not treat me. I felt I would pass away, for my elder brother had informed me that the earthquake had killed my father, and so would I. I could hear the people around me died one after another, moaning at the beginning, followed by heavy breath afterwards the voice disappeared suddenly, and then there came the crying…

My elder brother loaded me on the wheelbarrow again.

(In the afternoon of July 28ᵗʰ, on the road leading Tangshan to the airfield there appeared the returning crowd. This unceasing tide bombarded the continuous tide, converging a large flood returning to the ruins. The trenches along the road were filled with corpses; those push–to-the –wall people were wondering where they were going. However the airfield was still in the center of jam and blockage)

The Record of Interview (2)

There was only a small medical unit consist of 40 personnel in the airfield of Tangshan Air force. When hundreds thousands of refugees poured in, this tiny medical unit was like a small boat built with thin boards on the roaring tremendous waves. Every time the army doctor Shao Junlan and Wang Yalian recalled the situation on July 28th, they always had their hearts trembling. After the earthquake they ran out of their houses with flaws, hurrying up to the medical unit immediately. At the moment they could not imagine the miserable scene in the downtown area because only a small number of Russian style houses in the airfield collapsed. When the wounded people were sent to them from the nearby villages. They kept stanching bleeding, winding bandages, sending the wounded people in the ambulance to No. 255 Army Hospital as usual. However the ambulances to the 255 Hospital returned soon after they're starting, bringing the news that Tangshan had been flattened. Then a full load wounded people appeared first on the road. A moment later, a crowd and crowd of people struggling out of the ruins poured into the gate of the airfield with more serious fear…

Running about in circles, lifting all the war standby medicines, we cleared up the wounded, solidifying, injecting cardiac. The first aid medicine got less and less quickly in spite of more and more wounded people arrived. People were lying everywhere in the airfield, crying for help by stretching their hands. We wondered where we could go and how to manage.

Clutching constantly was blocking us. An old woman said with crying, "Doctor, please save my son, he is dying. If so I'll be left alone." A young man, pointing to a young woman said, "Doctor, please save her life, we have got married a few days ago." Also several tens of people were shouting, "We came from Guizhou province, we came from Guizhou." After some questionnaires we knew that they were from Tongren region of Guizhou province, all were officials over the position of the people's commune and the total number of them was 260, who passed Tangshan after visiting Dazhai and Shashiyu village, the survivors of whom only over 30.

What else could we do? We had cardiac and bandages first, only reserved Mercurochrome and tetracycline afterwards. The medicine boxes became empty at last; those wounded people, who seemed to imagine their lives could be rescued by any kinds of medicine, claimed even the atropine.

There was a boy of eight or nine years old who would never be forgot by us. He cried and shouted, "Aunt, come to save my brother, my parent have died, only he remains alive, please save him…" Beside him a boy of 12 or 13 years old was vomiting blood full of his mouth, which painted his chest red. After only glimpse we confirmed some of his body organs were badly wounded and were having internal hemorrhage. We had had haemostatic gone, to say nothing to have operating apparatus. The child suffered from shock, we could do nothing but clutching his philtrum with which we knew clearly useless, but went on desperately until his head lowered, body became cooler and cooler…

We almost had our hearts broken. Seeing those wounded people died one by another, listening to their shouting for help, tears came to our eyes but we could do nothing more. We had nothing remained. To the patients who suffered from anuresis, we had no catheterizing tube; to those fractured we had no splints, to those needing debridement we even had no anesthesia.

The debridement without anesthesia was deadly painful. A child of seven years old had a large piece of scalp lifted which was filled with sand and must be washed with salt water and cleaned with brush. Who could put his hand to do? The mother of the child said, "It is more important to save his life, to set about your hand." I still suffered from heart sick every time thinking that debridement. We washed the blooding and flesh blurred head, brushed slightly the sand debris mounted in the flesh. The child trembled every time we touched him, his mother shouted beside, "Their, and their. Do not fear pain you should be like the PLA man, be brave…" Clenching his teeth the child really did not cry, did not cry…

The wounded people became more pitiful when it was raining. A man with his face cracked and twisted remained walk, straggling in the rain. A very thin old woman wearing the midwife's clothing, penetrated back and fro in the bush. Of the wounded lying on the ground some were suffering from convulsions, some were moaning miserably, some were delirious from high fever. We found a bottle of oxygen, combining it to an unconscious wounded man. After a circle of running, we found a circle of people had lain around the oxygen bottle. We did not know how they had crawled here, nor how they found a piece of tube, which was connected to the bottle of oxygen, with which they sustained their lives…

There were also several tens of pregnant women to give birth. Some were dying here, and others were giving birth. I could not recall how we deliver these children.

The mothers of these children would never forget the airfield on July 28ᵗʰ.

. The Record of Interview (3)

Zhao Fu was a male nurse in No. 255 Army Hospital, a wounded having one of his arms fractured. Mentioning July 28ᵗʰ what he could not forget was the basketball field of the airfield. The tiny square piled up by wounded people and corpses.

Those people lay about the basketball field at sixes and sevens, among whom those dead people and living ones mixed. Generally those dead men were covered with towels and handkerchief on their faces. The living people were crying and shouting. Because my fractured arm was swollen, in order to reduce pressure the doctor cut one another flaws on it. I did not know pain at all at the time, only knew thirsty and hungry. Someone offered me a can of pears,

Cracking it to the ground, I picked up those pear pieces on the ground mixed with sand soil and glass fragments, plugging into my mouth. Beside me there was a corpse of a man at about 40, I rested my head on his chilly arm… lying there over a whole night with the corpse.

(Many people undergoing the earthquake have said that the night of July 28th had no even a

Single spark in the urban area of Tangshan city, as if the whole city had sunk into the pitch-dark bottom of the sea. The rain stopped but the sky was still compacted by the clouds heavily and starless. There were only few flashlights in the darkness, resembling the will-o-the-wisp in the graveyard. Occasionally there were few shrill and long barks, particularly sad and sorrow. Before the relief armies arrived at Tangshan, the city sank to a dead night, which acknowledged so many people what deadly silent meant.)

On the next day wondering how to fetch them we transferred those corpses to other places.

The relief armies had arrived Tangshan constantly. There were seas of people on the highways, always jammed. I heard someone shouting, "Let those vehicles carrying wounded people go first, those trucks loaded with grain go through the rice field." The trucks went and stopped in turn, loading more and more wounded people.

I dared not to recall the situation of these wounded people because it was too cruel to man. The earthquake was really merciless. Speaking of my passengers, a man had one of his feet lost, the skin of which was curled, exposing the white bone, only a piece of rope holding the huge vessel at the knee point, he kept crying on the way, tearing his throat. There was also a girl of her 20 years old, possibly had her spleen broken, every time the truck rocked, she cried. She asked to stop the truck, but how? She clutched my hand suddenly and said, "Comrade, I beg you. I beg you to beat me to unconscious so that I could no longer feel pain. It was too sore for me to withstand now…"

We were sent to an army hospital in Jixian county. Only hearing a soldiers crying, "Carry those alive ones here, those dead people there!" I fetched an army doctor and asked him to give operation. He said,   "How can we operate here? In the very day of yesterday, 1,400 wounded people died here. We could not manage, we could not manage."

By my glimpse there were people lying in and out of the hospital everywhere. The white-hot sun, the smell of the decayed wounds, shined them, as well the smell of soil stimulated the nose of people and flies flew about with booming. I lay down right in this hospital till the arrival of the sanitary train next day.

(During the one and two days after the earthquake, before the arrival of large number of relief armies. Those survivors breaking through ruins carried out self-relief tightly. Among the Tangshan survivors after the earthquake, eight tenth or nine tenth were rescued by their relatives, colleagues or neighborhood from the ruin. It was a common thing that one survivor struggling out of the ruin decided the fates of tens of people, who in turn decided other hundreds of people. It was extremely miserable that the Tangshan people carried out self-relief, rescuing each other, seeking life by themselves, organizing to transfer those wounded people outside. Those compacted broken trucks staggered out of Tangshan, passing through slowly and difficultly those vehicles and people confronting them. They were stopped constantly, unloaded those dead men who had puffed their last breath, often stopped by some other refugees carrying those dying wounded, who had waited along the road for a long time. (The Tangshan Military Region wrote down in the information of Anti-earthquake and Relief: A truck carrying full load of wounded people was driven to Yutian county. It was going on in great difficulty, as if having its steering wheel wrong, the wheel of which turned this side sometimes and other side a moment later; when on uphill road, it puffed black smoke, unable to go up longer. The truck arrived at Yutian County at last, the wounded people on which were carried down, some one summoned the driver to have a rest, but got no answer. Opening the door of the truck people were shocked to be stubborn, the driver was a heavy wounded man, with his head hurt, intestines out and left hand fractured. When people tried to carry him down, discovering he has passed away on the steering wheel, blood was flowing about the drivers cabin...)

Setting off for Tangshan, I carried a thick pile of notes with me. "Please look for XXX for me." "Please search comrade XXX." "Please questionnaire the situation of wounded and death of family XXX." My mother also asked me to search her close friend Jiang Yuchao, the director of the Civil Affairs Bbureau and his wife, Zhou Guilan.

Uncle Jiang, uncle Jiang was a man who watched my growing up. How lucky it was! When I began my first day of calling, I heard this familiar Subei (northern Jiangsu province) accent in front of the camp of Shanghai medical team. It was he, who remained alive. I ran up to him, standing before the old man who had his rib fractured and therefore bent his back.

"This young man, how familiar to me..."

"I am Qian Gang. Uncle Jiang..."

I was cherished at one blow by a pair of trembling hands.

"Tangshan...You just looks at Tangshan..." uncle Jiang burst into tears. For the first time I sensed the sore of a broken heart.

Above and On the Ground

About 200 medical teams hailing from every corners of the country, more than 10,000 medical workmen scattered on the ruins of Tangshan rapidly. One another Red Cross banners and wooden board wale stuck into the ruins.

Here is the General Hospital of Air Force

Here is the General Hospital of the Navy

Here is Shanghai No. 6 Hospital

In the afternoon of July 28th, there appeared operating camps to receive Tangshan wounded refugees in Hangu, Tianjin. At the very night the surgeons of the General Hospital of PLA had constructed three operating tables in Tangshan airfield.

These were the earliest operations after the earthquake, also the most difficult ones. WE conducted large number of debridement and sewing ups, large number of amputations, even opening one's head. All were done in an extremely simple condition. Wang Zhichang, a doctor of No. 255 Army Hospital joined in the operation in Tianjin medical team after sending wounded people to Hangu. He said he could never forget the reed mat shed built on the soil, they stood almost in blood to rescue those wounded people, with shoes soaked in blood. He had only one pair of operation gloves, which were washed by running water after one operation and then reutilized. However there was even no running water in Tangshan airfield, the nurses of the General Hospital of PLA, sterilized the apparatus by boiling the water taken from the swimming pool. The doctors operated the heads or caesarean operation under a gas lamp without blood plasma, the wounded died one after another on the operating table… Recalling the situation of the several ten hours beside the operating table of the day. Dr. Sun Yupeng said, "There were so many dying wounded people, whom we knew clearly hopeless, but also carried them on the operation table. Sometimes two hours operation was only for one hour surviving of the wounded." Every time mentioning Tangshan, Zhu Shenxiu, the orthopaedics first thought of the soil pit outside the operation tent, which was filled with amputated arms and legs…

Yang Lifu, the director of the hygiene department of the logistics department of Beijing Military Region and Liu Zhen, the vice director drove their jeep about Tangshan day and night. They could hardly concentrate the hundreds of thousands of medical personnel scattering the ruins but did the very thing themselves. When several tens of heavy wounded people of Fengnan County could not be transferred outside. Liu Zhen bounced on a skylark helicopter, flying to rescue them on the coast. The damage was not less serious than that was made by a cruel war: of the 18,591 wounded people transported to Liaoning province, various fractured wounded made up 50% of the total, paraplegia made up 9.1%, cartilage made up 17.09%. There was almost a heavy wounded among every five Tangshan wounded people, making a total number of more than 100,000.

"We must deliver these wounded people out of Tangshan." Liu Zhen said to the provincial party secretary Liu Zihou, "We will not be able to finish the operations if we did this way!"

Liu Zihou said, " Transfer the wounded people to every county in the province."

On July 30th the state council decided to transfer the Tangshan wounded people to 11 provinces and cities of China. Before issuing this decision only more than 50 wounded people suffering from lumbar vertebra fractured, leg fractured, serious extruded had been transferred to Beijing by the returning planes. After issuing the decision of transferring the wounded people to faraway places, large number of airplanes as well trains had been dispatched to the disaster region, starting the unprecedented transportation throughout the country.

By August 25th a total number of 159 trains (times), 470(times) airplanes transported 100,263 wounded people to Jilin, Liaoning, Shanxi, Shaanxi, Henan, Hubei, Jiangsu, Anhui, Shandong, Zhejiang provinces and Shanghai city.

In the first and second days of transporting the wounded people, Tangshan airfield was in a
jammed disorder.

In the deafening booming one another planes shoot into the sky, those busy people almost forgot those uncountable number of deadly wounded people were sent into the sky in a badly damaged airfield.

At the north end of the running way of the airfield, a broken control tower commander parked. Zhao Yabin, the dispatcher and other three army men in their underwear and straw hats on heads, sat in that broken commander vehicle, staring the sky with their eyes, commanding the airplanes' taking off and landing by the transmitter-receiver.

In the duration of half of a month from July 28th to August 12th, more than 2,885 (times) airplanes took off or landed at Tangshan airfield, during which the most busy day 354 (times) taking off and landing were done; on an average of one taking off or landing every two minutes. The categories of the planes were complex, the speed of which were quite different to each other, as well having such a density of taking off and landing. All of them, even an average day was astonishing deed to such a medium sized airfield, to say nothing to that it was in post-earthquake days when the aviating dispatching room had been damaged, plus the aftershock happened constantly.

Within the 48 hours after the 7.8 Ms earthquake, more than 800 aftershocks with Ms more than 3, among which those strong shock over MS 5 were 16 times, as well in such a disorder on the ground.

The air force was forced to walk into the blind alley. The airfield decided to utilize the commanding vehicle to command double taking off, while the dispatcher instructed the taking off and landing by range estimation.

The deed should be recorded in the history of Chinese aviation. A few young air force service men, boarding in the commanding vehicle day and night were ready to introduce airplanes all the time. There came the booming of engines of planes constantly, sometimes the number was even more than ten, appearing above the sky of the airfield. They called with their husky voice, adjusting the height of the passing of various planes; just like those policemen directing the endless traffic at the cross. Some other service men, running back and fro on the runway, more than 1,000 meters, leading the landed planes to reach the position loading or unloading people; sweat was dripping on their heads, walking constantly no less than 100 li (=50km) every day. It was they who enabled thousands of airplanes taking off or landing safely, even a slight friction had not been occurred among the airplanes or between planes and vehicles. It was also they who laid a road of rescuing wounded people and save those dying in the emergency moment, laying a road on which endless relief goods were transported to Tangshan.

It was also busy on the ground.

According to the recorded information by the front headquarter of Anti-earthquake & Relief Disaster of Hebei province. In the post-earthquake days there were more than 20,000 motor vehicles of military and civil took part in relief work. These vehicles, planes and trains not only transported the large number of wounded people in emergency but also transported the following goods to the disaster area: (by the end of the year 1976)

Grain stuff: 76,110,000jin (1 jin=1/2 kg)
Biscuit &diets 3,664.7 tons
Sugar   1,230 tons
Meat   947.1 tons
Vegetables   1,406 tons
Clothing   1,573,000 pieces
Shoes   410,000 pairs

Cooking apparatus 5,287,000 pieces
Match 6,110 cartons
Soap   11,652 cartons
Washing powder   32 tons
Medicine   293.7 tons
Reed mat   2,620,000 pieces
Straw bag   2,556,000 pieces
Wooden log 8,973,000 pieces
Bamboo stick 1,014,000 pieces
Iron wire   1,000 tons
Nails   1,030 tons
Asphalt felt 56,510,000 bundles
Asbestos tiles   364,500 pieces
Plastics sheet   1,043 tons

In the days living in Tangshan airfield I often stepped my feet among those piles of relief goods covered by plastic sheet. There were mountainous piles of flashlights, batteries, and hill-like piles of ship biscuits, piles of pans, bowls, and spoons; there was also Yunnan Baiyao (Yunnan White Medicine) sent by Yunnan province. There were also gift bags filled with towels and teeth brushes sent by Haicheng, Liaoning province who had suffered from earthquake… In the two post-earthquake days, the station director of the airfield (an officer of the regiment degree) dominated allotting all the relief goods and did not hand over to the commanding headquarter of Anti-earthquake &Rescuing Disaster until July 30th. The allotting work at the beginning was in great disorder, large quantity goods were overstocked or allotted blindly. I have visited Fengnan County where the vegetables were brought only one sort, the exported honey garlic. I had to eat a large bowl of sweet garlic for each of the three meals.

The primary disturbance was unavoidable. Although the Tangshan party committee had established the headquarter of rescuing disaster in the morning of July 28th on a broken bus, as well the headquarter of both Hebei province and Beijing Military Region had been established at the very night, confronting such tremendous disaster those officers with white temple of the party and government as well as those generals had not any experience to deal with such emergency. They shouted hoarsely by calling up, had their eyes bloodshot. It was until 30th of July, they did not carry out their commanding in some range. How many problems were waiting for them; water supply, power supply, communication, traffic and transportation. The nature destructed the city in few seconds, however it would take a long time to recover its prosperity by the people, the first batch of affairs to do were the followings,

Water supply: on July 30th, the 30 water tankers innovated from oil tankers by Beijing Heavy Motor Plant were supplied to the thirsty Tangshan as the first batch. There was still 3,300 tons of clean water in the water reservoir of Dahongqiao water plant of Tangshan Running Water Company. However all the major water supply pipes, about 100 km within the city were broken by the earthquake. On 31st July, over 12,000 hose was transferred from Shanghai by airplane to supply water to densely populated region.

Electricity, on July 28th, two generator trains were driven out of Beijing, supplying power to the commanding posts of anti-earthquake and rescuing the disaster located in Tangshan airfield; on July 29th the high tension line between Yutian county and Tangshan was recovered. On July 30th, it began supplying power to the water supply area of the city, the airfield and Kailuan Coal Mine.

Communication: the communication of Tangshan city was interrupted entirely after the earthquake. In the late night of 29th, the maintenance team of the post communication system of Liaoning province had recovered the telephone line leading the northeast three provinces passing Tangshan and communicating Tianjin and Beijing.

Railway: on August 7th with the emergency repair by the PLA engineering corps. The Beijing-Shanghaiguan railway opened to traffic.

No matter how many years passed, every time thinking about the night of Tangshan after the earthquake, the light would appear in front of my eyes, that yellowish street lantern, that magical street lantern.

Not only few Tangshan people had said in the second night after the earthquake a street lamp lit beside a path where the debris had not been cleared up. This was the only street lamp throughout the pitch-dark city, which was as gloom as a candle, as uneven as a candle, but extracting the sight of thousands of Tangshan people. Who on earth could have imagined that it was nine workers of a factory who lit it by revolving a hand generator raked from the ruin? In this deadly silence, how much calm and hope this street lantern had given to the still trembling people.

This was the unceasing light of life of this city.

Save Lives

The following is an extract of the "Bulletin" of PLA Daily. (Correspondent Xing Shicao, August 13th, 1976)

… The commanding post of Anti-earthquake &Rescue Disaster of Beijing Military Region held a meeting to summarize the work of half of the month. The vice political instructor Wan Haifeng delivered the summary and the extract of which was as followings: The total number of relief troops were 100,000, including Beijing Military Region, Shenyang Military Region, the Air Force, the Navy, the PLA Railway Engineering Corps, as well those Engineering Troops. By August 10ᵗʰ, these troops had saved 12,245 people…

In those emergency days, the most serious problem bothering the authorities of the party and the government, the soldiers and officers of PLA was the lives buried in the ruins. To save lives, this overwhelming task fell upon the shoulders of the ten thousand soldiers and officers of PLA.

Speaking exactly, in addition to those about 20,000 army men inside earthquake area, the first troop entering Tangshan were the No. 1 Battalion of the infant regiment of some tank division of Beijing Military Region who stationed in Luanxian county of Tangshan Region.

At twelve in the noon on July 28ᵗʰ, the No.1 Battalion had reached in front of the ruins of Xinhua Hotel of Tangshan by vehicles.

"The soldiers were astonished to be stubborn," Li Fuhua, the political instructor of the time recalled,   "Whoever had seen such miserable scene, the corpses, brain and blood lay about the ground, some soldiers could not help from tears coming into their eyes. I was worried, "What are you crying, to save those survivors." I had had my voice changed and its tone was trembling… We thought it too easy when we started, even did not bring a shovel with us, to say nothing to those large machines. Relying on their pairs of hands, the soldiers raked the debris of stone, shifted the slabs of buildings, and as well dragged the steel bars.

Li Fuhua could never forget the grief of soldiers when they were exhausted but could do nothing useful. The moaning, the shouting for help could be heard everywhere, but the remains of blocks of buildings compressed the countless rarely living lives as mountains.

A young man, stretching his head just out of a flaw of a piece of slab shouting, "Help, help. PLA man!" However the soldiers could not lift the slab even one inch. Tears in eyes, they heard the mechanical shouting of the young man again and again, becoming weaker and weaker, became hoarse and finally disappeared…

On one corner of the hotel, the soldiers heard the voice of a girl producing under the ground, "Comrade, here we are seven, seven people…" They raked downward desperately, having heard the breath of the girls. The earth rocked suddenly, some overhung slabs fell down; the breath ceased. After several hours, the exhausted soldiers saw the seven parallel lying female corpses.

In the afternoon of July 28th, two thirds of the soldiers of No.1 Battalion had their nails unshelled, having their hands' flesh gloomed with blood. These young soldiers, tightly closing their mouths without any word, desperately however low in efficiency raked the solid ruins with their blooding hands.

When the 7.1 Ms aftershock took place, we had sixty or seventy soldiers in a dangerous building. A company commander shouted,   "Hurry up to go out, the earthquake is coming up!" but none of the soldiers went out. By shouting the company commander himself exerted in,   "We must rescue these people out before the collapse of the building."

In the condition without any tools the battalion overturned the whole hotel completely, saved more than 50 people in and around the hotel. We rescued more than 20 people the next day, and only 4 or 5 on the third day. "Within the first three days arriving at Tangshan, our whole battalion had nothing to eat, to drink, and kept our eyes open. The meal sent from the barrack had been given to the fellow citizens, In the fourth day they boiled a pan of rice with the water from the bathroom, the smell of which made them vomiting and none of them had a swallow. In these few days, these men showed their astonishing mental and physical strength. They had their up body bared, only a trunk on the lower body, crashing the bodies with full of scars. They seemed crazy, only knowing raking, raking, raking…what they seized were lives! The commander was so worrying the he lost his temper. The soldiers were so worrying that they kept crying, but we had only pairs of hands…"

Recalling the relief in Tangshan, the generals confirmed it was a big mistake that they did not carry heavy machinery when entering Tangshan for the first day. It would have been better if

Large number of cranes had been transferred to Tangshan from Tianjin and Beijing. Those field armies might carry more steel rods, hammers, shovels etc. But be confronted the abrupt disaster no one could react rapidly in calm and deliberation. The troops sent to rescue disaster were actually an army without any weapons. It was until August 7th. The relief troops were not allotted cranes, electric saws, rock drills and electric welders. This was to say, this unprecedented cruel struggle between life and death on the ruins continued for as long as ten days with the bare hands of soldiers. When calling GAO Tianzheng, the political instructor of the army said such words with strong emotion, "In those ten days all our soldiers felt they grew up suddenly…"

The army of Gao Tianzheng executed the task to save the victims in Xiaoshan area of Lunan district and the area of Tangshan Railway Station where were most seriously damaged. Gao Tianzheng could never forget his young soldiers who were also the victims of the disaster, not only bearing the toil, danger but also bearing the heavy mental burden, "The hearts of our soldiers seemed to be struck by daggers at the time, in some places we could see clearly that someone was alive in the depth of one or two meters in the ruin. However we could not get in but staring our eyes. The people inside were suffering misery, so did our soldiers outside! The Red Army Regiment of our division saved people around the Railway Station, the second company was in charge of those in the buildings of the station; the third to those in the dormitory department of the railway; the fourth to the hotel in front of the station. Each company was in charge of a large area. What in front or them were those hard concrete slabs, steel bars. I still remembered that one of our political instructors found a pile of steel saw blades somewhere, with which they cut the steel bars, throwing those broken ones, in this way they broke up the solid reinforced concrete slabs…"

To those who were struggling in the ruins, the soldiers tried their best to send them food and water. They forked the steamed bread or apple with steel bar to plug into the ruin through the flaws of the ruin. A rank of soldiers had got another idea, to plug one piece of flexible pipe into the ruin, by which they fed the dying wounded people with boiled millet glue. The soldiers shouted again and again with their hoarse voices to inspire those victims to insist on.

When the heavy machines were brought, the soldiers became more tightened. It had been ten days, even if there were someone alive, the life of whom was at the very end. Some of the soldiers exerted themselves into the ruin the slab of which had been pried up; someone sitting in a small basket was lifted to the remained building by a crane. They searched people alive and saved them in various dangerous places. I witnessed a soldier in front of an inclined collapsed building. He was carrying a middle-aged man on his back, walking down step and step from the steep slope difficultly. What is the matter with him? He dragged a large piece of wooden board on his heel. Looking carefully, alas, he stepped upon the nail in the wooden board; the people down the slope were worrying about him. Carrying the man on his back, careless to the pain in his heel, he dragged the wooden board and went down, went down and down… with his forehead sweat through, the foot bleeding.

The living people saved from the ruins became less and less. The victims underground could no longer moan or shout. They could only beat the water pipes or thermal heaters powerlessly, to transmit weak signal to the people above. They organized "overhearing team" in Gao Tianzheng's army. When everything got silent in the late night, a rank of soldiers lain on the ruins, listening to the ruin by taking up their breath. Whatever a faint sound was heard; they blew the emergency muster whistle, doing a crash job to rake the ruin. The soldiers who were just fell asleep were awaken by the whistle, hurrying up the ruin, one another were driven to the pitch dark, snow white projector shone their rays upon the ruin. The motors of the crane boomed, the banging of the hammer aroused up and down. It was regular that nothing was found after the toil to dawn. Sometimes they raked for three or four hours, what they dug out was only a dying but alive chicken.

Were there any people alive under the ground?

Chapter III Life Seekers

Before men underwent the drown disaster it was difficult for them to imagine the meaning of life and recognize little what stubbornness and roughness they need to keep alive. Usually the passing away of lives not only replies on the external disaster, but also depends on the weakness of man himself.

Wandering in the streets ten years ago among the large number or piles of corpses, some bodies of the dead had aroused my deliberation and doubt. These people obviously did not die of striking or compaction. What left on their perfect bodies were strings and strings of dark red blood stain pitted by their own nails, which were prints clutched in depression.

"This was mental collapse." A veteran doctor going to Tangshan said to me. It was they who killed themselves in extreme horror.

Many dead people died this way. However proceeding their instinct of more stubborn desire to seek life, man stuck on strive magically for keeping alive and seeking life.

This wonder was not the only wonder in history of life, but also the wonder of psychological history of human being.

Tangshan earthquake, with its destroying and shocking test, engraved the names of these life seekers. They were doubtlessly the proud of human being.

Three Days, a couple and a banging kitchen knife

The husband was Chen Junhua, at his age of 24 years old, a staff of political department of No.255 Army Hospital.

The newly married wife of Chen was Hao Yongyun, at her 24 years old age, a commune member of a village in Langfang County.

The time of being rescued: July 30th, 1976, three days after the earthquake.

Three days were not too long to the limit of man's life, but to this couple, they were peculiarly long and unbearable. Their remaining alive was a miracle to themselves.

On July 26th and 30th, I called the couple Chen Junhua and Hao Yongyun. When talking with Hao Yongyun, their lovely daughter was playing by the bed, which sometimes turned her head back, staring curiously at her mum and me. Obviously she was born in the post-earthquake days. In the future this vigor petit innocent creature will know that she would not have been born to this world originally. Because the earthquake almost seized the lives of her parent who got married at that time.

The strong seismic waves of July 28th struck all the large targets, also smashed the small wedding room of this couple.

At the moment, the room was extremely bright and shining, as if the light were on. We felt the walls of four sides curled and collapsed like making dumplings. Our room was on the ground floor of the building, the ceiling of which had fallen down, leaving only a few inches from our heads. Luckily the ceiling did not fall to the bottom, we two put our arms around each other, and there was only a space as big as an armchair remaining for us.

When being struck down at the very moment, this couple had shouted for help. Their exhausted shouting was in vain to the tremendous ruin.

To seek the path to keep alive, they, as thousands of other victims at the time, pushed the beams desperately, striking the steel bars, lifting the stones. When calling Hao Yongyun, she said to me,   "My husband is a Man, a really Man. A screen door compressed his body, where did so large force come to him? He tore the iron wire of the screen door and was found by me his hands became bloodstained."

"It was like to bury men alive." Hao Yongyun said, "At the beginning, it was pitch dark in the surrounding and we could not see each other. We felt boring only, and were irritated, the mouth and the nostrils were plugged by dust. When there came the aftershock, the slab almost stuck our brow!"

The newly married wife was not strong physically. Chen Junhua told me, "She was poor in health also was suffering from neurasthenia". At the moment we were irritated seriously. I was very worrying about her. I was squatting while she was kneeling and bending over my body. She said to me constantly, "Junhua I am suffocating, I am thirsty."

. I   could cry thirsty madly only. It was extremely hot and I was thirsty deadly. Junhua asked me not to cry any more for the oxygen was scarce inside, which could be used up by your crying.

I could no longer withstand the thirsty, stretching my hands to touch all about. It was too dark, only I felt a bottle. Was it a bottle of vinegar? I was so glad, fetching it to pour some into my mouth. But it was peanuts oil. Drinking two swallows, I vomited all. When I became unconscious, I always saw a military kettle in my dream, which I held tightly.

- ➤ Seeing my wife's condition, I remembered there were watermelon, peaches and half of basin cool water in my room, in which a jar of Chinese herbs was immersed. I touched with my hands all around, but could get nothing. Everything had been crashed. In desperation I happened to fetch a kitchen knife, I said to my wife, "It is very good now, we can break our way out with this knife."

- ➤ This kitchen knife brought hope to this couple to remain alive in the honeymoon. In darkness there went the banging of the knife's striking on the solid ware. Chen Junhua dug a hole in a broken wall first. Madly pleased, he crawled outside, who on earth knew a cold hoarse cement concrete balcony blocked up the hole he dug. He chopped with the knife to the opposite direction, and also resulted in another failure. The petit space they temporarily inhabited was really like a tightened tomb.

- ➤ I chopped all the sides around me, stones, steel bars, water pipes and thermal heaters… the blade of the knife curled, turning into a triangle iron piece. I struck seven holes altogether, all of which were blocked holes. I wondered how much time had passed, only felt it was sound summer outside. It was too boring and too hot. I had my forehead swollen with my swellings. My wife only had a piece of underwear and a trunk, crying and not leaving me with one step, fetching me tightly. I moved near her, she began suffocated and unconscious. I touched a straw hat with my hand and started to fan her with it.

Every time she opened her eyes, she cried and asked me if we could go home, would there be anyone to come to rescue us. I was grief very much. There was no sound in the surrounding, only some booming or banging spread over our heads occasionally. Seeing her lying beside me, I was worrying with a heavy heart. Having got married newly, having had a family constructed for a few days. My wife joined me from her village to have our honeymoon, which has not last. Would we come to our end this way? At that moment I became depressed and got my heart bitter. At the moment of aftershock, fearing the ceiling above our heads fall, I padded it with many bricks. By this moment, I really thought to draggle these bricks out, waiting for the falling of the slab to murder us two together.

Somewhere not far from us there spread the gradually weakening crying of a baby, there was also the sound of rolling of a child, shouting "thirsty". This was the family of Wang Qinghai, our neighbor. Every time Chen Junhua moved a little, his wife would nervously had tic in faint. She clutched her husband's hand desperately, very tightly. "Have you seen the sky?" she asked. She was in hallucination, listening to the mechanical banging of the knife striking the hardware. Although this banging was grudging and mechanical, dull and powerless, still was she listening to the hope of keeping alive? "Have you seen the sky?" "Is there any hope?" Seeing his weak wife, Chen Junhua bore his depression. He knew that if he became depressed, it would mean death to her.

"As a result he said to her, "It will, it will. It will be dug through, will be through." " Can we break out? Can we break out?" " Yes. We can. We should, I assure you." Chen Junhua 's knife banged again, which was produced by striking a heater. No longer seeking the unexpected road of keeping alive, it was only for comfort his wife, for the weakening confidence of keeping alive; she should not pass away like this.

Distant relatives engaged their marriage. The beginning of their love story was not very sweet. Every time being mentioned, Chen Junhua felt some compunction and bitterness in his mind. At the beginning the first love letter written by the undereducated girl to him was written on the behalf of some other, which he knew later and lost his temper. He asked, "Why did you cheat me?" Yongyun cried for a whole day, just because of her undereducated she was too infatuated.

In the darkness the wife remained her crazy talking constantly, her breath became quieter and quieter in the banging of the knife. She told me later,   "Without Junhua, I would have died earlier. It was he who supported me."

It was entirely three days and nights. I would have died if I had been keen on death. I felt I was at my end the second day and thought what my parent would think of if we were struck to death? If we couple died together, it would cheat our parents. In fact we were keen on living."

Chen Junhua would have tears in his eyes for there was a trivial in his mind. Before they got married, Yongyun had been hoping to have a bicycle, the common desire as those citizens in the town. However they were so poor that they could not save enough money to buy one for them selves, but only bought one in cooperation with their younger brother, and rode it in turns with him. Chen Junhua had made up his mind secretly, they would lead their life frugally after wedding and the first thing to buy was a bicycle branded pigeon, possessed by himself entirely for his wife. The banging of the knife became weaker and weaker. Chen Junhua too, was exhausted. He felt serious fever throughout his body, and had his hands and feet powerless, probably because of mydriasis. He saw white fog around him. At last he lay down. However he remained striking his knife. Holding this small triangle piece of iron plate with its blade curled. He lifted it as lifting a large tripod of one thousand kilogram. Bang, bang, bang, the sound lasted for two days and three nights.

At six o'clock in the afternoon of July 30th, when the faint but stubborn banging at last spread out of the ruin, they were saved.

Eight Days, "Little Girl" Wang Zilan

Wang Zilan, a female at the age of 23 during the earthquake, a nurse of No. 1 Hospital of Tangshan. The time being rescued from the ruin: August 4th. The following was the extract of calling in Tangshan in August 1976.

On August 12th, the comrades in the head office of Shanghai Medical Brigade informed in the No.1 Hospital of Tangshan a female nurse was rescued by PLA men from the ruin eight days and seven nights after the happening of the earthquake, whose name was said Wang Yulan.

The confusion of the name had been corrected later. Ten years later when being called by me, she was working in the hospital, wearing a set of white uniform, hair in the white cap, coming into the office of the hospital director with smile. Her first words said to me were, " The PLA men were very kind. I still remember the names of the two PLA men, one is Mo Zhanjiang, and the other is Wang Fenglian."

At the time she and her colleague Sun Guimin were blocked in the treating room of the department of paediatrics and did not know at all that eight days had gone. According to their accounting in the darkness, only four days had passed. She asked me with laughing, "You asked me if I was frightened or not at the time. Hey. What would I be frightened about? We fetched a bottle of grape sugar salt water by touching with hands and drank some when we were hungry. I worked as a nurse, knowing we would not die, only it was not comfortable when drinking and I had my stomach burning. There were a lot of people upside, as well many foreign area accents by my judgment. I was very glad who else would they be but the PLA men; they were coming to rescue us. I kept waiting for them, falling asleep after drinking, faint and muddled. I underwent the disaster."

Was it really so easy to pass the eight days and seven nights for a girl like her? According to her own words, she had been a woman fearing death extremely. Being compressed under the ground, she passed her time among the piles of corpses. She said, "There were wounded people everywhere near me, the voices of whom were horrible, some crying with hoarse voices, some were breathing heavily, particularly those longing cry at the moment to breath their last, like some beast's roaring!"

In those eight days and seven nights, Wang Zilan heard clearly people beside her died one by one. When there came a blast and blast of bore gas, she smelled the unbearable stench, the corpses began rotten.
In mentioning what she had done in those eight days, she said, "I felt homesick, desired to break out, thought of those children in the paediatrics department; I also thought of him, who I knew for only three months. We were at our very beginning. Speaking to what else I did, that was to generate the Dongfeng watch, listening to the tick tack of the watch was a pleasure for me. I was afraid of the watch's stopping, generated it constantly. It was said the watch would become rusty if it stops. I liked the watch very much. It was bought by me when I attended to work."

In the eight days and seven nights, she had raked the debris of the bricks, lifting the wooden boards, having exhausted, having undergone the horrifying silence with her hair standing at their ends, undergone the darkness from which they tried to flee but failed. However what made her unforgettable was something interesting," I raked, raked, raked, but only raked a spittoon out." For which she chuckled unceasingly.

In the process of calling, what Wang Zilan talked about was the work and life of her today, her pleasure, angry grief and happiness among people. She was particularly keen on trusting others. Only several minutes after our conversation she had tears coming into her eyes for a confronting contradiction; afterwards she could chuckle for another interesting thing. I seemed comprehend her "simple and easy" eight days.

I could not help to recall the situation when Wang Zilan left the ruin. After eight days and seven nights when a deputy political instructor of PLA, risking his life got into the hole drilled by electric drill and lifted a large board of a table size compressing Wang's head, Wang Zilan after eight days being buried in the ruin straightened her waist abruptly, stood up like a spring. She was really an interesting girl. Her case was almost the only instance of all the survivors in Tangshan. When talking about this, she laughed again, "The more interesting thing was, because of my pleasure I remained calling the two PLA man "Uncle" constantly, who were of the same age as me, maybe younger than I."

I smiled too, inwardly. I recalled someone had said to me, the soldiers hearing Wang Zilan's shouting for help in the ruin had thought there were seven or eight cackling little girls being buried in the ruin.

. The Extracts of Notes of Calling Tangsahn in August 1976

It was said there were more people surviving their lives with the substitute food found in the ruins. The instances are:

A child of some district being buried in the ruin had a pillow in his arm. When he was hungry he tore the pillow with his teeth, chewed the sorghum husk to allay his hungry until the time being rescued.

A citizen in the ruin near a fruit store relied on the fruits to the moment being saved.

A citizen in some district after being struck in the ruin, it was a basin of wash-feet water that saved his life.

. Thirteen Days. A woman surpassed the Limit of Life

Lu Guilan at the age of 46 when there came the earthquake, inhabited in Xiaoshan district as a housewife.

The time being save, August 9th, 1976, thirteen days after the earthquake.

According to the record of medical documents, in the condition of running out of water and meal, the life limit of a woman was seven days.

On 13th August 1976 that was to say, the fourth day after Lu Guilan returned to the ground. I saw her in the tent of the medical team of some division of Beijing Military Region. She had wakened from unconsciousness just. According to the medical record, Lu Guilan had her leg fractured, blood pressure very low, and serious acid-poisoned reaction throughout the body when she entered the hospital.

However she lived on, keeping alive for thirteen days in the condition of running out of water and meal, the fact itself was a wonder in the history of life.

Before the spring Festival in 1985, with great expectation I found and revisited the old woman. What I could not comprehend was this magically appearing woman was almost forgotten by all. The various grades of administrative departments of Tangshan did not know her address and whereabouts. Finally I found her address among six similar names of Lu Guilan in the population archives of the security bureau of Tangshan city. I could not help to be puzzled. It has been ten years, no medical scientists; no institute of a hospital was interested in her, or carrying out investigation or research of her past and present. Regretfully I was not a medical worker and have not got even the modest essential medical knowledge. Therefore I could not make a detail explanation to the whole process that this old woman broke magically the limit of human life physically and physiologically. I regretted, but I believed in the content of her experience described orally. Even illogical, disordered would never be valueless to research of human being scientifically today.

However there existed great regret.

The followings were the extracts of my notes of calling, strange but genuine.

. When there came the earthquake I was accompanying my husband who had been suffering from cerebral haemorrhage and lived in the hospital four days earlier and was at his end that night.

A doctor said to me he had not any blood pressure. Not having answered his words there came the earthquake. Hiding under the bed of my husband, I was not stuck to death. When being buried at the moment I could not withstand for few minutes and was boring very much. I was compressed with a large pile of ceramic tiles on my chest that I wondered where they rocked. Being compressed to suffocating, I lifted the tiles one by one and finally could breath. I could not stand up at all, being buried inside in a gesture of shrinking my body and could do nothing. I shouted for help, but no one came. There was banging above my head, two soldiers were talking about. I shouted again," I was a woman, not a devil. My husband named Yang, who was a worker in the bathroom." But the men above me did not hear my words.

Exhausted with crying, I was very thirsty. Lying on my back, I dared neither to open my eyes nor my mouth. There came the second shock. I thought bricks and stones locked all corners. I could not get out. I imagined I could give the whole Tangshan city to him if it was mine on behalf offering me half bowl of water. At the moment of the second shock, I could not withstand any longer. How did I drink? I tore the clothing to pieces with which I soaked the urine to drink. I drank the second time many days after the first drink, which was much less and was very bitter.

How could I know this was earthquake? Damn it, "Dacheng, Dacheng." I summoned my son desperately and wondered what they were getting on with my daughter. I summoned Dacheng to come, to break the bricks for me; those weasels and hedgehogs compressed me inside. I was too thirsty and thought my daughter had passed away. The nice house of the hospital fell down, how could our small hut withstand. It was pitiful to my husband. What a miserable life he had led! He worked as shoes repairer from the age of 20 and was a very honest man. He died just above me. But I could not attend him upon his dying. The most pitiful things were my two children. I was afraid my daughter would not live longer. Who would come to save her? The woman of our neighbor was very bad. She would step her feet on her corpse if she saw, to say nothing to save her. She hated us. She would not come to save us. Mentioning the woman would make me lose my temper. She always bullied us, trying to seize our house and driving us out. She also told lie, saying I committed adultery. I could not account the number of days passed, only angry with the woman. For a moment I began faint, imaging her, a shovel in hand, passing by head. I shouted, but she did not save me. I was very angry and thought I should go out. I should insist on. Someone will come to save me. I should win this battle. In faint and puzzle, I heard many voices and sound, the sound of car and plane. Sometimes I kept a very clear mind and shouted, "Plane, my dad and mum, help me."   Again said to myself, "There. There. Do not be frightened." "Alas. I thought if I did not die. I would go out to see others. I missed them very much. If I have only one sight upon them, it is worthy to suffer from this disaster. Afterwards, I fainted more and more often."

You asked me if I felt hungry. How could I feel hungry when I was struck at the moment? How
hungry I was! I remembered I bought five-yuan (RMB) meal coupon the day before, with the second of which I booked a set of meal, in which there was ice and boiled round pork ball. In the evening of 27th, I bought two pieces steamed bread. Why did not I eat up the second one, which I knew just putting beside the pillow of my husband, which I tried to touch but failed. After a long time of touch I could touch a handful of clay, which I swallowed up because of extreme hungry.

I was faint at the time and in gloom I heard someone lift me by laying up bricks. I went out at last. It was said a slab as weight as 2000 kg was above me, which was hoisted and shifted by a large crane.

Sometimes I felt neither hungry nor thirsty, only feeling cold. I had drunk my urine for two days, which ended up finally. I was very cold, trembling from my heart to outside. I exercised my body desperately, not being able to stand up. I curled inside, rocking like a monkey. Afterwards I dragged a blanket, a green one, which I chewed with my teeth, trod with my feet, as last tore off a piece, with which I covered my body.

Sometimes I read the quotation of Mao Tsedong, "Make up our mind, fear not sacrifice…" singing, "The sky is big, so is the earth…" which I learned at the neighborhood committee. In those days I was faint now and then, faint and then woke up, woke and then faint, only a fly was accompanying me, the pitiful fly like me, who could not get out. The booming of the fly was so miserable and very loud, like the crying of a child. Oh. In faint I thought it like the crying of a child. I thought I would die, while the bad woman did not save me, even seeing my dying. It was lucky I had undergone dying tens of times. In the war, the bullet flew over my scalp and killed my first husband. Going to the well to carry water, I fell into the well and faint. I was fat but the well was thin, which clutched me at the middle. Only half of my body fell into the well as the iron handle of the well platform struck a scar on my forehead. This was the most serious accident of all. By this I could not move any more and had nothing to eat and drink.

The husband died in the hospital was my third one. You asked me why I am so strong. I trained up my body with bitterness. I got married at the age of 16 and became a widow at 17. How did I know cold and hot? My husband had died; I should present gifts to my father and mother-in-law. I toiled desperately, like a young man. What a life a young widow would lead together with her father and mother-in-law, even having a bowl of glue would be treated with disdain of them? I only knew work unceasingly. Chopping sticks, I did not go home until the stars were in the sky. Carrying the load of 100 ji (50 kg) on my back with one blow, walking for tens of li (1li=1/2 km).   The sticks chopped one day would be enough to burn as fuel for a month. I was able to drive a cart. It was only I, who worked as the cart driver and was very powerful. When being thirsty in work, I bent my body over some trench to drink water, never fell ill. I feared neither hard ship nor having glue made of corn flour with salted vegetable. I remarried another husband at 22, who was a patient and died only three years later after marriage. A coffin cost two hectoliter corn, which I made by selling cotton shoes. What a miserable life I had led. It was said "to be a widow, she will not have cotton pants." I had been to several families where I lost my husband and remarried. I married the last husband when joined the cooperative but the earthquake killed him again.

Lying there I thought of these things in faint. Afterwards I could no longer shout. I said to myself. There, there. Do not worry. Do not worry. I will wait for going out whatever happened and surely be able to. No matter how long it will be. Thinking in this way, I got my tongue drought at last, which was as tough as a lump of clay. I tore the skin of it making it bleeding, from which I taste some moist.

You asked what my sensation was in faint. What sensation did I have? I saw a large cast iron bell rusty, just as the bell in the primary school, which rang all the time unceasingly and making me boring. I thought I would be saved when the bell stopped ringing.

At 7 o'clock 20 minute p.m. August 9th, 1976. Beside the ruin of the Commercial Hospital, when a large crane lifted the slab as weight as 2,000 kg, there came the wonder, all kinds of journalists and TV photographers had filled Tangshan, a crowd after crowd people were staring at scene of rescuing Lu Guilan from all the viewpoint. It was told by a soldier witness that she could not move any at the moment. However when the two soldiers raked the clay compressing her eyes no sooner she opened her eyes than she shouted, "Long Live PLA." It was truly a wonder. In the condition without water and food, having spending 13 days in the ruin. Lu Guilan remained a clear mind. I heard afterwards it was in the duration when Lu Guilan was treated; an accident occurred and nearly killed her because of the poor quality of some medicine. However Lu Guilan again beat the medicine accident and remained alive stubbornly.

I have been required doubtfully, "Among so much datum, why did you choose the disordered talking of this old woman?" I have deliberately earnestly and always think, being able to remain alive for 13 days in the ruin, apart from her strong body of a laboring woman. Lu Guilan also had some psychological factor of a rank-and –file Chinese woman. If the misery fell upon an intelligent woman, would there be the wonder of 13 days?

I spent the eve of New Year of 1985 at the home of this old mother. Seeing again this old woman excited and inspired me. What I was astonished more was, although being limp in one of her legs. She remained the spirit as before. The old woman not only took part in the public work from being a housewife, also like many young ladies bought a mini wheeled bicycle, running back and fro busily on the Tangshan roads.

This is life. This is the power of life. This is the life and the power of life of a rank-and-file Chinese woman.

Fifteen days, the Last Five Men

Chen Shuhai at the age of 55 during the earthquake, the site squad leader of Zhaogezhuang Mine.

Mao Dongjian 44, the vice group leader of excavating group.

Wang Shuoli, 27, the group leader of excavating group.

Wang Wenyou, 20, a new miner.

The time being rescued from the pit was August 11th, 1976, 15days after the earthquake.

On Feb 5tth, 1985 I went to visit the five men who were rescued last during the earthquake in Zhaogezhuang Mine, where had burst the famous anti-Japanese strike led by Jie Zhengguo. It looks it was a place where there were many heroes. I only met three on the day; Wang Wenyou has been transferred to other unit. The most respected old man, old miner Chen Shuhai had passed away newly.

At the home of Mao Dongjian, I saw a photograph of the five men, which was taken by the journalist of Xinhua News Agency when they returned to the mine from the medical team. The background of the photo was the head frame. The five men were in sets of miner's uniforms, wearing the miner's helmets with lanterns, tying the broad miner's belts, stepping the up-to-kneel rubber boots, winding snow white towels around their necks. Although they were rescued not long ago, they had not any trace of having undergone huge disaster. Apart from the keeper of the photo, Mao Dongjian appeared little shy and nervous in front of the camera, all of the other four-manifested heroic spirit. Chen Shuhai had a broad face and a stubbly beard, having a pair of warm trustable eyes, some profoundness, dignity and strictness penetrating his smile. The strong man Wang Shuli in his most prosperous years, stood with his legs apart, strong and calm, a standard figure of miner. These two young miners seemed forgetting their weakness of having wept in the pit. Particularly the short man Li Baoxing, whose uniform was so long that reaches his kneels also raised his big head high, framed his thin shoulders, spreading his arms, manifesting the gesture of a hero. He was too thin and short, the whole set of costumes of the miner seemed to compress him down. He said to me, "I succeeded my father's job to enter the mine. I like the mine."
Such five men wrote a page of specific style in my notebook for calling.

The Selected Notes of Calling

July 28th 3:42 –18:54
At the time of the earthquake, we five were excavating at the surface No. 0597 near No. 10 tunnel. If you ask how deep the tunnel is. It was about 1,000 meters underground. On that day Chen Shuhai worked as the group leader. No sooner he had checked our squad and urged us "pay attention to safety" than there came the earthquake. We were excavating the coal, hearing the banging of the earthquake feeling it's rocking, by which we could no longer move. The coal of the No. 9 surface was dry, which fell down to form dust blinding our sight. The columns in diameter as big as basketball broke easily. All the holes of floating coal were blocked.
Wang Shuhai, "Is it the blast of gas?"
Lao Chen, "The blast of other surface would not influence ours."
Lao Chen, "Perhaps it is the pressure from the old roof."
The power in the tunnel was off, so was the valves of spraying dust. What could we do? We must break out. Where could we go? Upward? Downward? Lao Chen was very experienced and disagreed with the idea to go upward. He estimated that the upper, the more collapse there would be. What about going downward? If we went down the lower vertical groove for 8 meters we could reach the No.2 middle tunnel of transportation.

We five began to cut the vertical groove, which was blocked entirely by coal. The shovels could not be used efficiently. We used our helmets, carrying coal one helmet after another. Only one man could be sent to work inside. We ordered Xiao Li and Xiao Wang working in shifts. Wondering how hard we worked, keeping working from morning to six in the evening, the vertical groove was cut through at last. We asked the thinnest Xiao Li to set down, who shrank and frightened, was kicked down by Lao Chen. After his glance at it, he assured that the transportation tunnel was blocked, too. At 6:40 p.m., there came the aftershock blocking the vertical groove having been cut through by a whole day's toil, with coal falling from the upside. The ten hours toil was abandoned by one blow. The more terrible thing was three of the five lanterns went off at the moment.
"We can not go out. We can not go out."
Xiao Li and Xiao Wang cried, sobbing.
Wang Dongjian was sighing again and again.
Wang Shuli said, "Lao Chen. What shall we do? What can we do? How injustice would it be

if we die without our skin broken! Lao Chen was sitting dully, saying nothing.
They were suffering from thirsty, tired, very despairing, extremely despairing, particularly these two youngsters moved no longer whatever happened.
Chen Shuhai spoke at last, "We cannot wait for death."
"Go upward, which was the only path. The first destination was that used transportation tunnel, No. 1 middle tunnel."
They obeyed Lao Chen, confronting the huge disaster. They needed a backbone; He was rich in experience, as well our walking map.
We began our work in shifts. It was Lao Mao and Lao Zhao's shift and they would shovel coal with large spades, raking through the vertical groove upwards.
On July 28th the Zhaogezhuang Coal Mine had organized large-scale search to those five missing miners. When the searchers came to the No. 10 tunnel, they found the tunnel leading to No.597 surface blocked, shouting again and again, banging the metal supporting, but got no reply.
July 29th (28) 18:45---(29) 15:00---(30) 4:30
Lao Mao and Wang Shuli at last broke through the path leading upwards, to which they kept working from the day before to 3 o'clock in the afternoon of 29th, taking more than 11 hours.

The No. 1 tunnel was a used transportation tunnel, which was narrow, only was as wide as 1.5 meters. Because of earthquake many metal supporting jacks had been bent. At some points of the tunnel only one squatting man could pass even before the earthquake. It was like a gate of hell. At this moment, there were piles and piles of rocked coal in No. 1 middle tunnel, whoever knew they could break through.

They had not had any water for 36 hours, which made them very thirsty and unbearable than the day before.

We drank the urine of ourselves, which we collected, with our hands. The two young men Xiao Wang and Xiao Li vomited.

There came another terrible thing, one of the two lanterns became ruddy, only one gloom light as candle remained. Lit by the lantern of Wang Shuli, we came in front of the "Gate of Hell". The gate was closely blocked by wastes, as they expected, their expectation broke again.

What else could we do? Chen Shuhai said, by great pressure, the metal frames compressed down, the waste above might be loose, raking at this upside, where would be space. Lao Chen ordered Xiao Li and Xiao Wang to scale up to work. But these two went down soon after they got up.

Xiao Li said," I can do nothing with it."
Xiao Wang said,   "it is waste and it is too hard."
Chen Shuhai lost his temper, "We should not stay here waiting for death! You have got neither your skin broken nor your flesh blooding at all!"
Li said, "I can not do that…"
Chen, " you Fool…"
 Li, "Why don't you work if you are not a fool?"

These two young men were really worrying, in fact, how would they ask Lao Chen to work, who has had a miserable life over half of his lifetime, suffering from many diseases over his body. If this walking map torn, who of us could break through?

Wang Shuli continued his work. The waste was really hard. Raking a flaw they made their way in harshly, with which his belly skin was scared and hands bleeding. He lifted one another lump of waste desperately, simply marching inch by inch. Right at working, his lantern became gloom and ruddy. The pitiful light only remained a light point as big as that of a match. All the people got nervous, their eyes stared at this point of light. which at last went off. It was pitch dark, in which one could not see his fingers even if he put the in front of his eyes.

"Lao Chen." The lantern went off." Wang Shuli cried in despair.
 Without lantern it was just like a man without eyes. How could they break out alive if they did not have eyes?

At the moment Li Baoxin had a glance at his watch, it was four thirty. It was 4:30 in the morning of July 30th, from when they could only imitate time without watching watch.

4:30 July 30th

Tears came to Wang Shuli's eyes. Xiao Wang and Xiao Li burst into wailing, sitting down at the very site, crying. What could they say? Despair? Sorrow? No complain would do.

Mao,"My big family relies on me. How can my crowd of children survive? The youngest of them is only one year old."
Lao Mao was very grief. He formerly worked on the ground, to make 20 yuan or so more money, he volunteered going down the pit. He desired to have a son in his life, but the former four were all daughters, the fifth was a son. Carrying his son in arms for only few days, he would die here, how miserable it is! He cried and said, "I am afraid my wife could even not see my body."
Wang Shuli, "If I die. What can my wife do? Will she have her life with her father and mother-in-law at the age of 26? Or remained bringing the children up? The older son was only 6 years old, while the youngest was less than one year, who even does not remember my face.   The government will take good care of them if I died, but no matter how good care from the government will not be better than a man beside her. My wife has a very tender heart. When I wanted to work in the pit before and have crawled out of piles of corpses when meeting with the roof fall. She said that we would rather work in the countryside where we have what we earn, which were safer. I met with several roof falls since I went to work in the pit, only in one of which I had my arm dislocated. My wife cried and said, 'How can you meet with such accident if you plough land in the countryside. If you were chopped by nickel in harvest in autumn, only a small cut will be left.'"
Xiao Wang missed his granny. Mum has died, so has dad and the stepmother remarried. His granny brought him up. Usually when he went to work, his granny would see him off for a distance when work was off late, she met him far away at the cross.
Xiao Li thought of his father and wondered how anxious his sick father would be.
Lao Chen was silent and said nothing he was deliberating.
Wang Shuli stopped crying, he suggested studying Chairman Mao's quotation,   "Make up our mind, fear not sacrifice, and overcome thousands of difficulties to win victory!"
Chen Shuhai began to speak, "We must scale up, only go up alive will make both our authorities and kinsfolk easy."
As a result, we restarted raking inside. It was too narrow to shovel, but we could not wait for death, we should keep alive.
August 2nd or 3^{rd,} the accordance to assure time: Wang Shuli, "Perhaps we have been in the pit for a week."

"We finally broke through the 'gate of hell', the first batch of passengers were Wang Shuli and Li Baoxin and Wang Wenyou.
We three first passengers led by Wang Shuli draggled the water pipes and cable, scaling up to the No.9 tunnel through the coal hole. Walking and walking we stepped water under our feet which made us very pleasant; we bent over to drink the water in rail afterwards we went on touching ahead. Lao Chen and Lao Mao also followed us after breaking through the 'gate of Hell'.

All of us touched the tool room where there was a telephone. We called up but it remained silent. Damn it something must go wrong otherwise the switchboard would never be stopped. On the other hand there were not anyone in the No.9 tunnel. We sat in the tool room waiting, waiting for a long time. What could we do?

At this time Lao Chen could no longer remain calm. He began sighing and sighing, "Alas. I will retire and have the labor insurance next year but suffering from this event today, to which neither the God nor the Earth could help." However he had the backbone and said, "We should go out without stopping and go wherever we could reach." Along the railway Wang Shuli took the lead.

We were exhausted at the moment. Xiao Li constantly fell down to the pools with one step deep and another shallow and a layer of skin were peeled off known to us later.

Lao Mao pulled two pieces of straw mattresses from an empty engine, he was very careful, perhaps prepared for the unexpected accident.

As the power was off, it was impossible for us to go up in the elevator and could only through "the road of mule" which we had reached but unfamiliar to all, to be zigzag and rough to walk on.
None of us were powerful to walk and we sat down.

There was the noise of water like the roaring of oxen in the tunnel by which we could estimate the water had drowned the no. 10 tunnel. We could no longer delay and must go ahead of the water. We must go now. Wang Shuli said, "Perhaps we have been in the pit for a week?"

"No." to relax our mind, Lao Chen said, "It had not been for a week, isn't it always dark?"

"Dark?" Wang Zshuli said, "Isn't it always dark in the pit?"

We restarted our difficult scale. The vertical height was as long as 300 meters. Going up the inclined road, the stairs was long as 800 meters. We had been exhausted long ago and had had nothing but drinking the water in the rail. These 800 meters long stairs would murder us.

Tired, hungry, exhausted we exerted ourselves desperately.

It was August 6ᵗʰ or 7ᵗʰ. The Accordance of this time: Li Baoxin, "It is harsh to walk over these 800 meters which took us four or five days."

"We climbed up from No. 9 tunnel to No. 8 tunnel. We should exert our great effort to scale every step of these stairs. We found a stick to which every one held tightly. As walking we shouted constantly, "Xiao Li. Xiao Wang, hold the stick.""

We missed our road after we scaled 340 steps where there was a platform and we wound around and around and wondered how hard we have done to find the aiming steps. There were also other platforms for every other 340 steps to each of which we touched for a long time to break out.

We would take long time rest for every several steps we scaled. If we five had not gathered, we would be afraid none of us could insist on. You asked me what reaction we had in our bodies. Alas. The sensation… our heads were so heavy that we seemed to catch heavy cold, the stomachs were disturbing, the bellies became shriveled, the intestines were cooing, our hearts were beating violently and abnormal sweat went through our bodies…

It was too hard; we took four or five days to walk over these 800 meters.

Xiao Li, Xiao Wang cried one after another, in which their tone even changed.

(? --- August 9th) The accordance of this time: In order to recover production some miners were sent to the pit in Zhagezhuang mine on August 9th. A young miner has heard the voices of people but fled because of being frightened.

"The time when we reached the No. 8 tunnel could not be ascertained. But according to the former estimation, it would be August 6th or 7th.

After climbing "the road of mule" of 800 meters, we were absolutely powerless and wondered the exit from the No. 8 tunnel to No. 7 tunnel.

Lao Chen said, "Let's go to touch the train."

We touched the passenger train, getting aboard and laid down.

Our sensation at the time was paralyzed. We thought we would die whatever we did, just waiting for its coming. Lao Chen was afraid we would have got into a blind alley and began to talk to us.

Wang Shuli said, "If we could scale up, the first thing to do is going to the dining room. It would be better if there were newly cooked steamed bread. If not, having some glue will also do. If also not, it would do when we pick up some tomato or cucumber debris."

Li Baoxin, "If we go up, whatever we have will do, even if there is only corn flour bread and green onion, we could eat and drink enough food and water. It is really unbearable only to drink cold water."

Talking and chatting, we found there was lantern in distance, to which we shouted, "Come here, we are of No. 5 excavating district!"

The light of lantern disappeared suddenly, as if to be scared back. We could not find its shadow when we followed up. Later we heard that to recover production, some miners were sent down the pit, one young miner of whom entered the No.8 tunnel and heard the voices which he thought of devil's and frightened away.

August 9th---August 11th

These were the last three days before being rescued.

Lao Chen said, "We could be rescued if we remain alive."

Cold, extremely cold by which we were frozen stiff. We five men squeezed into one carriage. Apart from one stood sentry to observe the end of the tunnel and waiting for the light coming, the others put arms around each other because all of us had little thermal energy in our bodies. We did not know time at all at the moment. We had not have any sleep by the time and knew we could not and should wait for by opening our eyes.

At 12 o'clock in the noon of August 11th, when we knew later there came our men, a ray of light flashed towards us directly. The man in lead was old Luo, Luo Fuchang, and a staff of the technical department. We rushed upon together, rushing upon with crying. But at that time we could not produce any voice, having only breath but no voice.

Lighting upon us with his lantern, "Aren't you the miners of No. 5 excavating district?" Lao Luo asked, "Do you know what date is today?" " No. None of us know that." " It is August 11th, it has been half of month. We think you have died days before. We do not think you are still alive!"

It had been 15 days. None of us thought of that. None of us thought of that!

It was in the afternoon when I left the Zhaogezhuang mine under the winter sunlight, one another blackish mountains made of waste resembling one another chilly and silent pyramids, the sharp top of which could be seen by me until the Rome car drove me away.

The calls to these life seekers going out of the ruins ended. But in exciting I had untellable profound regret at the same time. When I returned to the urban area of Tangshan by car, passing through the streets where piles and piles of corpses had been located, this regret became heavier and heavier.

I thought of a dead, a girl named Feng Chengbo, thought of her unfortunate death, thought of the tale of her, too.

She was a nurse in the No. 255 Hospital of Land Army. When there came the earthquake, she was on duty in the ward of the ground floor. The three-storied building she was in fell down completely. After one day and a night, someone broke through several layers of slabs and raked a hole, finding she was alive. But a huge slab clutched her and an iron bed, the lower part of the bed inlaid into the debris of stones, while the up part of her body remained entirely good. She kept standing in this gesture.

The comrades-in-arms raked the debris desperately, lifting the timbers. However they could not shift the slab. At this time no cranes had been brought to Tangshan and all the shovels and picks were useless. The young body of Feng Chengbo seemed to be clutched by the jaws of devil, and could not be moved at all.

She was only twenty, all her comrades-in arms wept.

"Will amputation do?" someone asked.

"No." a surgeon said, "Without blood transfusion condition, she will die as soon as she was amputated."

Feng Chengbo seemed not hearing this conversation. For a day and night she was exhausted by the torture of her wound. With a pale face and the head inclined on the elbow of her arm, she still smiled slightly to her tearing comrades around. She said nothing, only waiting. Before she went to duty that night, she had bathed. Her fluffy black hair had not been combed in time, hanging down her white dress of nurse. There was nothing more miserable than that a witness' seeing a girl's dying. Someone, enduring grief, sent half of a piece of watermelon and fed her with a spoon. Her comrades-in-arms had had their hearts broken, getting into the petit hole, accompanying her in shift, taking care of her. Xiao Feng looked not to be able withstand longer and fell unconsciousness again and again.

"It was too cruel." One of her comrades told me. When Xiao Feng opened her eyes last time, her comrade Zhang Shuming was just beside her.

"Xiao Feng, what else can I do for you?"

Feng Chengbo tried to say something but could not produce any voice. Zhang Shuming understood. Tears in her eyes, taking her ten fingers as a comb, she combed Xiao Feng's loose hair. Everyone knew Xiao Feng was a girl fond of her own beauty. In that age the appreciation to her was not very good. It was said her major shortcoming was "fond of her own beauty, not being hard and simple, keen on washing with a piece of perfumed soap and wearing her hair in bangs etc." It was on that day this lovely beautiful girl passed away after her comrade combed her hair. "She looks quite quiet. Looked like falling asleep, falling asleep forever." Due to that immovable slab, the body of Xiao Feng was left at the site for days. She seemed to be alive. The girl could not dress herself as she liked and on her heart's content. However she was beautiful when she said farewell to the world.

I seemed seeing her last gesture, an extremely beautiful petrified girl. How can you say that she has died?

In the history of man's life, the physical death is unavoidable. However their mind can surpass the limitation of death; some victims having their mind broken, killed themselves by their own hands, but many people like Feng Chengbo died unavoidable; carrying a milestone of victory that man's mind overcame the devils of death in the ruins of disaster.

Chapter IV In Another World

In The Hotel
(Nippon Jiji News Agency, Tokyo August 1st)
  Title The Bone Ash of Sunaga Returned Home
  Sunaga Yoshiyuki (27) of the Neo Japan Commercial Company who died of the attack of the earthquake happened in Tangshan Hebei province China on 28th last month has been brought home by his wife Karashi together with three other his kinsfolk at 4:20 on August 1st airliner 800 of Iran Airway.
 Karashi, carrying her husband's ash, in a black dress, supported by her kinsfolk at both sides got down the gangway ladder of the airplane and was met by 50 of her relatives as well colleagues in black gauges.
  The newspapers abroad also reported before and after August 1st.
 Nineteen of the Teacher's Delegation of Greenland, Denmark left Tangshan safely.
  Twenty-three of the No. 6 Delegation Visiting China from the French-Sino Friendship Association left the earthquake affected area safely except one victim from France via Hong Kong.
  Three of the nine Japanese technicians who aided the construction of Tangshan Dohe River Power Plant died of the earthquake…
  There were a total number of 50 foreigners who underwent the unprecedented cruel earthquake in Tangshan on July 28th.
All of them settled down in Tangshan Hotel.
Tangshan Hotel was cracked in the early morning of July 28th.
  Two hours ahead of the earthquake, those French, Dane and Japanese were too excited to fall asleep for the attendance to the performance by Tangshan children; gathering under the fan of the rest hall of the hotel, drinking beer or soda water in the rarely high temperature, talking and laughing loudly. What lovely Chinese Children! But they were most impressed by those rabbits with long ears acted by those children. They went to their rooms after one o'clock, a.m. and could not fell asleep by those lovely rabbits, but were awaken by that suddenly coming noise roaring like lions and tigers.
  These were horrible sounds of earthquake, the banging of collapse of the buildings!
  The No. 4 building where Japanese inhabited collapsed from top to bottom.

The new building where French, Danes lived was rocked to have countless flaws. Although the structure of the building had not fallen down, there were many dangerous phenomena in the building; the slabs fell, the doors and windows changed their shapes, the stairs broke… Zhao Fengming, the director of Foreign Affairs Office of Tangshan, Li Baochang, the department director recalled that they were blocked in a small room the door of which could not be opened on the first floor of the new building at the time. The only pass for them was the window.

"Let's jump down the building."

"Go!"

The glasses of the window were broken with banging. There came the heavy sound of compacting of the two men. Zhao Fengming had his ankle fractures, he asked Li Baochang carrying him on his back, hurried up to look for translators and guards. Rescue those 51 foreign guests living in Tangshan Hotel immediately.

There spread the noisy moaning and shouting for help in foreign language in darkness.

Zhang Guangrui, the interpreter, shouted constantly in English, "Ladies and gentlemen, this is a serious earthquake. Be quiet. We are doing our best to rescue you all and ensure your safety and lives. Do not jump down the building. Do not jump down the building! Please link the curtains and sheets to a line and slid down the windows…"

A string and string strange safety belts hang down the twisted windows. By the instruction of the interpreter some of the foreign gusts had begun sliding down the window. Carefully and no sooner than there feet stepped the ground than the Chinese staffs of foreign affairs served them immediately.

"Hurry up, to be far away from the building." At this moment Li Baoxing was dashing into the building with others. They climbed up the broken stairs, stepping the shaking slabs, knocking every zigzag door open, looking for those wounded people or those victims not being able to carry out self relief. Several old Danes shrinking in the corner of the room and drawing cross over their chests, as if seeing the life buoys in the fierce waves on the sea. A sobbing old Dane woman put her arms abruptly around Li Baochang, with feet bared, Li Baochang supported the old woman first, then carried her on his back, carefully stepped on the glass fragment and reinforcement.

On other side, the No. 4 building of the foreign guesthouse could fall down anytime and was in emergency for help.

"We should rescue these foreign guests on whatever cost."

At this moment how many rank-and-file Chinese people just fleeing their death and broke their way out of ruins were affected by the above-mentioned idea. They ran into the dangerous area where the foreign guests lived, searching in every corners of the building, shouting and running the risk of their lives.

Li Baochang and others reached No. 4 building and put a ladder on the precarious wall. On the first floor actually the fallen third floor, the Japanese Hiraoka was lying, bleeding under the broken wall. Li Yunchang of Tangshan Safeguard Region and Xiao Cui, a policeman of Tangshan security Bureau climbed up together, Hiraoka's face was purple and dark, a slab struck his pelvis heavily. Not being able to carry him down, the rescuers bound him with a blanket, each end of which was tied with a sheet. Slowly they slipped him on the ladder leaning on the wall, and the people, down met him carefully.

Hiraoka shrilled by the fierce pain. Li Baochang shouted loudly, "Do not care for his pain, the most important is to save his life."

Another foreigner was rescued from the hand of devil.

An hour later, the relief high tide in the hotel became quiet temporarily. All those foreign guests hailing from all corners of the world have never forgot this day undergoing in China. Still are they stimulated and horrified when they recall all these today. On the strange territory, they became real refugees over one nigh. Being watered by rain, they sat down on the small square in front of the ruin of the hotel. With a flowered curtain on their back, and a piece cotton quilt on their heads of four, they sat in circle around a small bonfire made of wooden debris dipped with some kerosene.

They were in cold, thirsty and hungry, apart from which there was also difference from their races, as well the friendship and selflessness among the people in different religions.

The Chinese picked up small and green apples from the apple trees in the hotel, which were served as breakfast. What was regretful was there was no water to wash, no knife to pill. No. It was unnecessary. What could we be fastidious now? All of us were victims of the disaster. The foreigners were talking in Chinese in sign language. Cleaning the apples with the sheet, they swallowed them up, the sore and pucker taste of which would be unforgettable ever their lives.

A Dane female doctor cleaned the wound of a Chinese interpreter; bending over to the ground, another Dane friend laid sheet for a newly coming Chinese wounded. In rain and wind the weak Japanese sat back to back with French people, supporting each other; more and more people were taking care of those moaning Japanese badly-wounded.

There were still three Japanese missed.

Exhausted Li Baochang raked their way into the ruin again with others. He suddenly found a group of French and Danes following him, the leader of whom was Miner, at the age of 60, who was the leader of French Delegation visiting China.

"We too, want to look for those Japanese."

"No. No. It will not do." Li Baochang was confused by this unexpected situation, "Please go back."

But these foreigners stepped on the ruin.

Li Baochang shouted via the interpreter, "You are not permitted to attend, do not attend. Your surviving is the most comfort to us. We should not allow you to be wounded the second time."

Several young foreigners ran ahead of them after untying the hands holding them.

A French madam ran up, too, untying her high heel shoes and handed them to Li Baochang, pointing to his bleeding bare feet.

Everyone recalling this scene thought it was a moving one; on a stretch of ruins, those white race people, yellow race people organized actively a collective to rescue the dying people and conducting relief those wounded people. Beside them there were broken pillars and wall, which might fall down anytime; above their heads there were shaking beams. However they had forgot all but knew only these few dying lives. They forgot pain, forgot time, and forgot their location. Forgot the difference among their nationalities. Everything was blurred at the moment.

Li Baochang, wearing a pair of French high heel shoes was shouting and issuing orders. The French Dane and Chinese people were searching the trace of the Japanese. They found them finally; the Japanese experts Tadokoro, Yoshikayu and Takeuhaka had died, and the badly wounded Sunaga.Yoshiyuki died too after sent to Tangshan airfield.

In the afternoon of July 28ᵗʰ, the Ministry of Foreign Affairs of the People's Republic of China decided to send an airliner to Tangshan to meet these foreigners.

Two cars ran to the airfield from the hotel like wind and lightening.

As every vehicle met with on July 28ᵗʰ, they were blocked on their way by crowds of wounded people. In front of the drivers there were old men, children, heavy wounded… countless eyes for help.

"These are foreign guests." The driver's mouth became puckering with heart trembling,   "These are badly wounded foreign guests. Let me go."

These are our kind and faithful Chinese people. When hearing the two Chinese characters "Wai Bin" (foreign guest) the shouting for help and abusing stopped immediately. The Chinese people always take politeness and righteousness over all and succeed this national style one generation by generation.

The Chinese retreated silently, although they were getting fierce pain in their legs and were supported by wooden sticks. When they moved one step, every moan of the wounded in the wheelbarrow being pushed away struck the hearts of their relatives; they were still giving the way.

The several tens of foreigners received the same highest honor in the airfield. In the starving July 28th, they were served with a cup of valuable rice porridge and a piece of thick, hard fried cake to each of them. At last in the green uniforms offered, blue pants and "cotton shoes of old men" by the air force, they got aboard the plane. Tears came to their eyes. Holding the blood stained hands, they asked again and again,   "You are still wondering what they are getting on in your families, aren't you?"

"What about the Kailuan Coal Mine?"

"And those little friends acting as the young rabbits, where are they now?"

These foreign guests have not forgot those lovely Chinese children. Just like today the Tangshan people are talking these foreign guests full of emotion.

In front of the gate of modern Tangshan Dohe River Power Plant, there is a long stretch of Japanese cherries blossoming, resembling a piece of light ruddy cloud floating gently. These Japanese cherries were planted to memorize those three Japanese victims died in the earthquake. Ten years later, when I walked on the former ruins I often hear people talking them in a sympathetic mood. It was true, they were very good friends. They cherished faithful feeling to Chinese people. Their strictness and industriousness impressed their Chinese colleagues deeply. Sunaga, working as the Japanese-Sino translator spoke fluent Chinese. When he talked and walked with the Chinese workers, he resembled a real Chinese. He had been to China aiding construction three times, the last of which was a long departure after the honeymoon, only one month after their marriage. He came to Tangshan… How affecting his death would be! The chief representative of No.1 expiry project Tadokoro was a turbine expert of Hitachi Corporation, before the earthquake he was having his vacation and had delivered a telegraph to his wife, inviting her to join him, visiting southern China and having sightseeing to Sanxia (three gorges of the Yangtze River). He also prepared a gift for his wife an elegant porcelain vase. After the earthquake, people raked out his suitcase, in which there were all the fragments of the vase. His wife took all the fragments to Japan and asked some craft man recovered the vase, putting on her bed table, watching it every day and memorizing him too.

However what else the dead people had carried away? Which was unknown by all in that era. Only those workers of the Dohe River Power Plant remembered with great regretful feeling. In

53

the Spring Festival before the earthquake when the Japanese and Chinese people held a banquet to celebrate the holiday. The Japanese electric engineer Takeuhaka put forward a suggestion suddenly; he would mobilize a movement of "signing names" and asked every Chinese friends having shed sweat together to sign their names on his notebook as memo. The Chinese became blank, the Chinese in 1976. The workers stared at the authorities of the plant, which stared each other and then went out in silence. They should ask for instruction from their authorities, whose answer was, "You must make it clear what their aim is, otherwise you should not sign…" The Japanese friends put their notebooks back to their pockets, regretful, unexpected, misunderstanding… Tadokoro asked friendly, "Japan and China have establish foreign relationship, why do you refuse even sign your names?"

Regretful. Just like the unrecoverable vase forever.

I would not like to criticize the answer from the foreign affairs office here. I even sympathize and comprehend them. In China of that time, in China in 1976, weren't there more such questions and answers from authorities?

It was quite even, in that uneven year.

In the Lockup

"Rattled. Rattled, Rattled…"

"Rattled. Rattled. Rattled…

In the early morning of July 28th, a string rattling of rifles echoed above the sky over Tangshan lockup, which had cracked to be a stretch of ruins earlier.

Several soldiers breaking their way out of the ruins, having their heads bleeding issued a string warning with a squad used machinegun shooting into the sky, and hasty fierce rattling of the rifles.

In front of them, one another prisoners raked their ways out of their prison rooms even in sleep, had gathered to a crowd by the shooting of the guns, wondering what they would do.

The huge wall with live wire entanglement collapsed.

"Stop. Do not move!" the bleeding machinegun man was shouting, the essence evolved through a long experience of an army man made him stick to his post at this special uneven moment, He shouted again and again, "Anyone can not step out of the former boundary wall. Take the live wire entanglement on the ground as the boundary."

The former strict guarded lockup with two gate guards had been leveled to ground.

The steel made gate lay down on the earth, the watchtower had fallen to a pile of stone debris; almost all of the more than 200 prisoners, watchmen and guards were buried in the ruins and broken walls. No voice could be heard from the felonry carrying instruments because of their inconvenience to move, most of them had been compressed to death. There were heavy noises from the female prisoners rooms, all of them remained alive.

About more than 100 people raked their way out. The field of vision widened suddenly, at this moment they stared at all these scene having not seen for a long time but changed thoroughly, the gloom head wheel of the mine, the top of the Phoenix Hill… But they could no longer recognize those streets, lanes and buildings familiar to them before. There were black ruins everywhere, a stretch of disorder, and a stretch of dreary. If there had not been the rattling of the bullets in the sky, people would have thought the lockup, the cycled microcosm like steel bucket disappeared from the world.

"Do not step out of the boundary!" the wounded guards were still roaring at the top of their voice with banging of the gun. Those prisoners not forgetting their status were standing, trembling and dared not to move one step. Out of the guarding boundary, several guards were staggering along, back and fro to rake out or carry those victims in a muddle.

From another would around the lockup, a wave of shouting for help spread over this special world louder and louder. The crying of women, the weeping of children, like foaming wave of the sea surrounded and dashed this isle like land occupied by these prisoners.

Some disturbance arouse among the prisoners, several of whom were murmuring something; three of them walked over to the guarding boundary by pushing and giving way to each other
After a moment of silence, one of them at last encouraged himself shouting to the guard, "You Honored Judge."

The guard honored as Judge did not hear the hoarse and trembling voice at all.
"You Honored Judge!"
The voices from the three drew attention from the guard at last.
" What are you going to do?"
"All of the people here selected us, selected us to require you… if we can go out to rescue these victims…?"
The shouting for help in surroundings became more and more grief and sorrowful.
The watches and guarding troops held an emergent meeting immediately. This was a special situation.   "What else shall we think of? There were so many people whose death and life are glooming. Rescuing them is an over all task. However in front of their faces there is a strong relief troop." The prisoners were organized into three groups.

"All Attention." The guards declared the disciplines loudly,   "When you go out, you should rescue those victims faithfully, which is an opportunity for you to perform meritorious service to atone for your crimes. Anyone will be put down if he tries to runaway."

The prisoners stepped out for the first time of the live wire entanglement falling down to the ground since their entry.

This was a special relief troop who was inspected by the bayonets.

The wounded army men led the wounded prisoners, those wounded prisoners in turn rescued desperately the dying lives of those rank-and-file people in the ruins, the first of whom were those officials and their family embers of the lockup, also those neighbors in the nearby street and lanes. Those prisoners like all the relief men on the ruin were in muddle and extreme hurry. They seemed forgetting their status completely, like all the rescuers, carrying those children carefully out, supporting those frightened-to-dull old men. Every time they raked out those corpses of the victims, they could not help from sighing slightly. They made desperate efforts again and again, raking, lifting and carrying. Their hands were blood stained; sweat and the rainwater flew down their faces, blending with mud. When lifting some heavy matter they roared sonorous work songs.

"Hurry up, there is someone crying!"

"Be better hurry, carry here a board of door."

"Come here, come on the old man is dying."

Several prisoners circled Gao, a cook of the lockup, who was having steel dark face, seeming to cease breath. But they still had the string of hope. A young prisoner arrested for theft did not give up mouth-to-mouth breath until they ascertained he had died. They covered Gao, the cook with a towel and ran to the place where there was shouting for help.

"The dormitory of the Court, the dormitory of the Court!" the guard was shouting.

"Doctor! Is there any doctor among you?" the people were crying. Mr. Wang XX was a doctor, who had committed as a hoodlum when on duty. At the moment, he bandaged the wounded, fastening fractured limbs constantly, as well shouted the principle of carrying out first aid to those wounded people. As soon as he heard the groaning of a deputy director of the lockup, he came up to him.

The deputy director was newly rescued who was struck to stiff; however do not forget his responsibility in his pale.

Seeing the prisoners running about he could not help from shouting,

"Come on. Come on. Call up the authority of the security bureau of the city. We are in emergency here. Oh! Oh…"

He moaned, whose bladder was wounded and could not withstand the pain at the time. He rolled over the ground painfully.

There was no cauterization tube.

Someone went back to look for the substitute tube, but he was made bold when he returned with empty hands. Mr. Wang XX kneeling beside the deputy director was sucking with his mouth on the ground there was a beach of blooding urine.

It was a whole day the troop under the bayonets did not take a rest at all. The prisoners were toiling without any words. Only few words conversation could be heard occasionally.

"It was more serious than the earthquake in Haicheng."

"Why there was no forecast?"

"Alas. I wonder what are things getting on in my family."

In fact these few bayonets could not control these prisoners scattered on the ruin, however they did not forget the invisible guarding boundary.

It was not until the night was getting the Tangshan security Bureau was getting ready to send these prisoners to other place. They did not find that three of the prisoners had been lost. These three criminals after rescuing the victims in the surrounding, desperately fled home to rescue their kinsfolk, two of whom returned to the lockup in giving themselves up after they finished their relief at homes. The other was busy about the ruin of his home when the motorcycle police arrived.

When the criminals were rescuing those victims on the ruins around the lockup, the staffs of it had began transferring those heavy wounded soldiers, officers and prisoners. The security officer Tian Guorui took a measure considered dangerous at the time, the driver was a prisoner, and so were the three "nurses" looking after the wounded people.

He could do nothing but this, the dying wounded people needed treatment badly, all the prisoners of the lockup needed to be transferred to a suitable place. They only found a poor Gass 51(an old SSSR truck) truck without driver. At the moment Tian Guorui seemed to be set on fire on his body, walking in circles around truck when Gong XXX, the criminal of hoodlum was looking at him.

"Mr. Tian. I'd like to have a try if you permit!" Tian Guorui looked at Gong XX, whose face expressed nothing, neither his pair of cool eyes. He seemed hesitating for a long time before he issued his idea. Tian Guorui recalled the young guy was a demobilized soldier and worked as a driver in the army, having driven over many dangerous roads and was a man fond of adventure.

"They would die." Seeing Tian Guorui did not answer, Gong pointed to the moaning wounded on the ground. "All right." Tian Guorui made up his mind, "You should be careful, this is an opportunity for you to make contribution."

The truck was started. This was an uneven trip. On the board, three criminals were looking after that blood stained wounded people. Among them the deputy director of the lockup being sweat through by pain and a squad leader with one finger fractured was inspecting the three criminals with alerting sight. In the cabin Tian Guorui directed the road with one hand, while the other hand never left his model 54 pistols on the waist.

The hospitals in the city were ruined. Wounded people filled the Fengren County of near suburb. The truck ran northward and northward.

Gong stared at the road carefully. In order to reduce pain by rocking, he wound those pits and lumps wherever he met. He tried his best to drive stably with neither any rough acceleration nor braking.

It began to rain, what dense raindrop, which flew into the carriage of the truck, by which the wounded people were cooled to trembling.

Someone was knocking at the ceiling of the cabin, "Mr. Tian. Mr. Tian, they will be frozen."

The shouting man was a criminal named Li who was arrested for swindling. He reached his head out of the carriage and said, "There is a barrack ahead of us, and I have got some people familiar there. Let's me go to borrow several coats."

Tian Guorui could no longer hesitate, the deputy director was moaning by both pain and cold. He permitted Li's going but warned him strictly not to flee.

Until Li ran over hastily and came back in despair Tian Guorui had not been able to imagine what had happened.

Mr. Li lowered his head sorrowfully; his comrades-in-arms would never believe that a criminal would be sent to borrow army man coats. Whatever Li explained was useless, those soldiers even observed him with alerting sights, at last he returned.

No one knew who was the most shocked by the event.

Li said nothing but remained silent.

Tian Guorui abused boldly, "What damn you doing?" his face tightened, no one knew whom he was cursing.

The truck went on ahead, the wounded people on which were sent to Zunhua County.

At night their truck returned to Tangshan, but could not enter the city, blocked at Xibeijing, loaded with crowd of wounded people.

"What can we do?" Gong asked Tian in a weak voice.

"What else can we do? There were large crowd of criminals and wounded people in the lockup, but it was useless whatever Tian Guorui worried about. "Go to Zunhua County again."

In the late night, the old model Gass 51 truck breathing heavily was driven out to Zunhua

County under the foot of Great Wall. Gong had had nothing all day long, driving his truck continuously. He began faint; eyelids touched each other in spite of his effort to open. It had been for a day and night, raking out of the ruin, rescuing those wounded people, long distance driving… neither eating nor drinking, having no rest. He could no longer hold the steering wheel; the truck began staggering on the road.

There came a haste sound of braking.

A man whose face was blood stained lay beside a compressed bicycle. Both Gong and Tian were awakening from their sleeping. Gong shouted in almost a crying voice, "I have compressed him to death, I have committed another crime over my old one…"

He rushed up to the man madly. When he and Tian found that the man was only wounded on the scalp, they carried him on board, sending him to Sunhat County.

Tangshan went to her bore hot July 29ᵗʰ in such disorder.

Tightening, tiresome and fear had tortured Gong and Tian Guorui weak over their bodies. The Gass 51 truck went back and fro on the highway between Tangshan and Zunhua, seeming to break up possibly at any time, Tian Guorui looked at Gong's pale and emotionless face constantly, puzzling in deliberation.

There had been such shortest dialogue.

"Hungry? "

"Yes."

"Thirsty?"

"Yes."

Arriving at Xibeijing, Tian Guorui and Gong got down the truck, bending over a wastewater pool, drink full belly of water. Tian Guorui found some fried corn sticks, holding in his hand Gong and he began pinching in shift.

The deadly starved Gong remained wordless when chewing, seeming to stay in his status as a criminal. Tian Guorui thought of why he was arrested; a pregnant educated-youth committed suicide with which he had committed sexual intercourse.

One day later the Gass 51, which Gong drove, became a police car on which guns were laid. He drove himself and other criminals in the lockup to the temporary lockup in Yutian County. When getting down, Tian pulled him aside in complicated emotion and said after a long moment, "Stay here silently and do not move about, the guards will hurt you if you do so."

At the very night when the criminals were sent to Yutian County, an event of camp blow up occurred.

No sooner than those exhausted criminals for two days fell asleep, a guy shouted suddenly in his dream, "The earthquake. The earthquake." All the criminals jumped up in fear, fleeing about. The fear compacted in their mind released at the moment. They plunged their way of seeking life without intelligence. The guards and watches shot their guns, shouting to collect them for a long time, calming them from fear.

Tian Guorui, the department director of Investigation and Criminal Research of Tangshan Security Bureau, interviewed me in his office, which was a middle-aged sharp, talkative man in a hoarse voice. Various documents were piled over his desk; he looked busy, with the little black rings around his eyes. I wondered why afterwards often thought that he had brought the fatigue nine years ago when he set off together with Gong.

This was the eve of Spring Festival in 1985. All the metropolises over the country were carrying out a movement to attack the hoodlum criminals. Looking out of the windows of the director's office to the gate, the police cars in blue and white were running in and out frequently.

Tian Guorui recalled the event of the year, almost not opening his notebook, he told those criminals who had made contribution, deducted expiry in imprisonment, or being released after the July 28th earthquake, as well where they were working or what they were getting on. In his narration this director whose responsibility was summing up the function of executing law and researching the legal theory lost his mind constantly.

"Tangshan earthquake was unforgettable to us." He said to me, "It taught us many lessons. To myself the most important was that the personality of the criminals should be respected like all the others…" I listened to him to finish all his words with respect. I saw anther layer of strength among the power in this very powerful law executor, which was more profound, broader and nobler…

Psychiatric Hospital

In the morning on July 28th, when the pharmacist Li Zhongzhi of Tangshan Psychiatric Hospital staggered out of the gate of the ruin, trying to carry a woman wounded lying slantingly under the tower of high tension wire on his back to a safer place, he was mistaken to be a mental patient by two miners of Kailuan Coal Mine, who shouted to him loudly.

"Put her down!"

"Put her down for me!"

The thin and short Li argued loudly, "I am a good man. I am a doctor."

He handed the woman to the miners and plundered the large hammer from their hands.

"What are you going to do?"

"To rescue people, our hospital has been leveled."

It was entirely leveled; the Psychiatric Hospital was leveled thoroughly. The ruins here were much quieter than anywhere else. There were steel bars in both the doors and windows of the wards, when the ceiling fell down the patients had no way to escape. Even if there were some survivors, they became unexpectedly silent; there was no crying, no shouting.

The first survivor fleeing the falling pharmacy was busy on the ruins lonely. He struck the big hammer, cracked the slab, rescuing more than ten staffs and children. He then led the slight wounded people rescuing the patients.

A young female patient who was good at martial arts raked out of the ruin, standing in front of Li Zhongzhi. She even had not been wounded at all, as well showed particular clear mind.

"What are you doing? Doctor Li?" asked she.

"I am rescuing people."

"I'll follow you."

Li Zhongzhi could not manage her. Dr. Zhang Zhiyong, Xu Jianguo had arrived from their rooms, together with the other staffs of the hospital. They rescued the patients one by one, carrying, lifting some times even draggling powerfully. A female patient refused to leave the blood stained debris of bricks and tiles, repeating constantly, "I am guilty. I should be put down. The ward has fallen down. I need not to wait for putting down. I'll wait for... I'll wait for..."

This was not a crowd of normal people. Soon later when more and more patients gathered together, Li Zhongzhi realized the seriousness of the matter. These unfortunate mental patients were entrusted by their kinsfolk to the hospital, as well to the state. They should be protected well. We would not let them run away like that woman good at martial arts, nor let them into accident... However the authorities of the Hospital were either died or wounded, none of them was attending.

The short and thin Li Zhongzhi was so worried to cry. He was a demobilized army man, only having been a health man and a pharmacist, not having instructed anyone. He looked at Dr. Zhang Zhiyong, also a demobilized army man, because of committing "rightist mistake", he split uniform as an army doctor, the same like Li Zhongzhi, an out-and-out cipher.

The ciphers held a meeting and decided to found the "leading group of anti-earthquake &rescuing the disaster of the Psychiatric Hospital." The staffs selected Li Zhongzhi, the only communist party member among them to be the group leader.

Li Zhongzhi sent somebody to ask the party committee of the city.

The city Party Committee replied, "Your authorities could no longer manage. You your selves organized resisting the earthquake and rescuing the disaster. The only principle is not to scatter."

Li Zhongzhi put the special heavy load on his shoulder, several tens of wounded staffs, several tens of mental patients, so many lives of people.

The doctors and nurses made a large circle with rope, in which they asked the patients to sit.

In the first three post-earthquake days, the lunatics behaved unexpectedly silent and obedient. Without steel bars or binding belts, they quietly and calmly sat in row, shoulder to shoulder. The remote ruins and corpses nearby would have stimulated them. They seemed having recovered over the night. From morning to night they only kept watching those going back and fro doctors, eating up the noodles sent to them silently, cleaning up the bloodstain on their bodied. At first those who took care pf them were only those unmovable wounded people.

When the aftershock happened, shouting arose around, but they reacted nothing, as if all were expected.

In those three days many healthy Tangshan people became mental patients, People sent these bold sighted language disordered kinsfolk to the hospital. These fiercely stimulated pitiful men murmured the names of he dead relatives, trembling constantly; some of them plugged mud into their own ears, some always tried to strike their heads against the electric pole. Their arrival increased the disturbance of the psychiatric hospital. The leading group decided to set up the temporary out patient service, receiving those new patients.

It was too busy and disordered. The thin and short Li Zhongzhi seemed to be smashed by the burden. He himself did not know whether his wife and daughter alive or dead who joined their relatives in Dongkuang (the east mining) district. However he had to serve the patients whole-heartedly. Had the medicines in the pharmacy been raked out? Had they allotted medicine s to the patients three times daily? There were also problems like meal, water, and the construction of shed from rain, to bury the corpses… Li Zhongzhi ran back and fro, falling down to the ruins many times. He felt his chest boring, wasn't his heart disease recurred?

Just as he felt weaker and weaker at the fourth day after the earthquake almost all the lunatics in Tangshan Psychiatric Hospital had relapsed. As soon as the counter reaction made of heavy stimulation disappeared, the silence crashed. They sang and danced, fought and in turmoil. There were those who refused to have medicine; who struck their fists; who toiled about; who cracked cups and bowls… together to make great disorder.

A middle-aged female patient having one of her arms fractured rushed out of the guarding ring, running in the yard. As a result, more and more patients like shied horses, shoot their bodies, stepping the limbs of other patients running out of the rope circle.

"Block them. Block them."

Li Zhongzhi shouted in his lean and hoarse voice. "None of them would be let go!"

All the doctors and nurses ran to the ruins to block the way of these starting patients, even those wounded who were bandaged and sticks in hand ran over, they shouted, cried knocked down by the patients, rose up again, snatching the clothing of the running patients.

When those patients were finally blocked into the guarding circle, Li Zhongzhi felt black in front of his eyes.

After a long moment, Li Zhongzhi found he was lying down the ground, one another glooming faces were looking at him and he heard the familiar voice of Dr. Zhao.

"Zhongzhi… your heart trouble… medicine…"

The short and thin Li Zhongzhi thought he would pass away, he felt he had been breathless, had not heart palpitation, and even had not hands and feet. He spoke something with a faint voice, which someone made it clear, that he would summon all the members of the leading group around him to hold a meeting.

This rank-and-file cipher would like to cry only in front of his colleagues, but bore it stubbornly. The first slogan put forward after the founding of the leading group was "not to cry" (not to shake the army's morals)

"Comrades, we should unite together, we should persist on, we should not scattered…"

"Zhongzhi, you should persist on, too. It doesn't matter. We are here, there is also medicine…"

Tears came at last out of Li Zhongzhi's eyes. He sensed tears from his comrades dropping on his face.

The relief troop decided to transfer the mental patients to outside by vehicles, while the "leading group" sent Zhang Zhiyong in charge the task.

The patients were making turmoil, the truck was rocking when Zhang Zhiyong looked at distance with a depression appearance… it was a zigzag road, a rough road. He suddenly thought his life was full of similar hardship. In time of "Committing mistake and leaving the army", he referred his expectation on the northern part of the country and hoped to have his latter part of life quietly led in Tangshan. However the serious earthquake made him suffer.

The End

July 28th, 1976 Catastrophe in Tangshan
"7·28" 劫难在唐山
Photographed by
Yaodong Kongpai